T0214722

Understanding Azure Data Factory

Operationalizing Big Data and Advanced Analytics Solutions

Sudhir Rawat
Abhishek Narain

Apress®

Understanding Azure Data Factory: Operationalizing Big Data and Advanced Analytics Solutions

Sudhir Rawat
Bangalore, India

Abhishek Narain
Shanghai, China

ISBN-13 (pbk): 978-1-4842-4121-9
https://doi.org/10.1007/978-1-4842-4122-6

ISBN-13 (electronic): 978-1-4842-4122-6

Library of Congress Control Number: 2018965932

Managing Director, Apress Media LLC: Welmoed Spahr
Acquisitions Editor: Smriti Srivastava
Development Editor: Laura Berendson
Coordinating Editor: Shrikant Vishwakarma

Cover designed by eStudioCalamar

Cover image designed by Freepik (www.freepik.com)

Distributed to the book trade worldwide by Springer Science+Business Media New York, 233 Spring Street, 6th Floor, New York, NY 10013. Phone 1-800-SPRINGER, fax (201) 348-4505, e-mail orders-ny@springer-sbm.com, or visit www.springeronline.com. Apress Media, LLC is a California LLC and the sole member (owner) is Springer Science + Business Media Finance Inc (SSBM Finance Inc). SSBM Finance Inc is a **Delaware** corporation.

For information on translations, please e-mail rights@apress.com, or visit www.apress.com/rights-permissions.

Apress titles may be purchased in bulk for academic, corporate, or promotional use. eBook versions and licenses are also available for most titles. For more information, reference our Print and eBook Bulk Sales web page at www.apress.com/bulk-sales.

Any source code or other supplementary material referenced by the author in this book is available to readers on GitHub via the book's product page, located at www.apress.com/978-1-4842-4121-9. For more detailed information, please visit www.apress.com/source-code.

Printed on acid-free paper

Table of Contents

About the Authors

Sudhir Rawat is a senior software engineer at Microsoft Corporation. He has 15 years of experience in turning data to insights. He is involved in various activities, including development, consulting, troubleshooting, and speaking. He works extensively on the data platform. He has delivered sessions on platforms at Microsoft TechEd India, Microsoft Azure Conference, Great India Developer Summit, SQL Server Annual Summit, Reboot (MVP), and many more. His certifications include MCITP, MCTS, MCT on SQL Server Business Intelligence, MCPS on Implementing Microsoft Azure Infrastructure Solutions, and MS on Designing and Implementing Big Data Analytics Solutions.

Abhishek Narain works as a technical program manager on the Azure Data Governance team at Microsoft. Previously he worked as a consultant at Microsoft and Infragistics, and he has worked on various Azure services and Windows app development projects. He is a public speaker and regularly speaks at various events, including Node Day, Droidcon, Microsoft TechEd, PyCon, the Great India Developer Summit, and many others. Before joining Microsoft, he was awarded the Microsoft MVP designation.

About the Technical Reviewer

 **Zain Asif** is a freelance senior developer specializing in Microsoft technologies (C#, ASP.NET, ASP.NET MVC, ASP.NET Core, Azure Data Lake, Azure Data Factory, SQL Server and Power BI). He is passionate about new technologies, both software and hardware ones.

He is the founder of Falcon Consulting, and with it, he has had the opportunity to work with the biggest companies around the world such as Microsoft, Canon, and Accor. His aim in the future is to make his company an IT engineering company and work as a freelance software architect and Microsoft expert.

When not working, Zain can be seen on the ground playing cricket or football or in front of a PC geeking and gaming.

Introduction

Azure Data Factory is the de facto tool for building end-to-end advanced analytics solutions on Azure. It can handle complex ETL data workflows and integrates natively with all Azure services with enterprise-grade security offerings.

For ease of authoring and to make you more productive, it offers a drag-and-drop user interface with rich control flow for building complex data workflows, and it provides a single-pane-of-glass monitoring solution for your data pipelines.

Something that really stands out is the low price-to-performance ratio, being cost effective and performant at the same time. Its data movement capabilities with more than 75 high-performance connectors are extremely helpful when dealing with Big Data coming from various sources. To give you an example, 100GB data movement would cost you less than $0.40 (that is correct, 40 cents). ADF is an Azure service and bills you in a pay-as-you-go model against your Azure subscription with no up-front costs.

ADF also supports operationalizing existing SSIS packages on the cloud, which is helpful if you are modernizing your data warehouse solution over time with a lot of existing SSIS packages.

CHAPTER 1

Introduction to Data Analytics

The demand for Big Data analytics services is greater than ever before, and this trend will only continue—exponentially so—as data analytics platforms evolve over time. This is a great time to be a data engineer or a data scientist with so many options of analytics platforms to select from.

The purpose of this book is to give you the nitty-gritty details of operationalizing Big Data and advanced analytics solutions on Microsoft Azure.

This book guides you through using Azure Data Factory to coordinate data movement; to perform transformations using technologies such as Hadoop (HDInsight), SQL, Azure Data Lake Analytics, Databricks, files from different kinds of storage, and Cosmos DB; and to execute custom activities for specific tasks (coded in C#). You will learn how to create data pipelines that will allow you to group activities to perform a certain task. This book is hands-on and scenario-driven. It builds on the knowledge gained in each chapter.

The focus of the book is to also highlight the best practices with respect to performance and security, which will be helpful while architecting and developing extract-transform-load (ETL), extract-load-transform (ELT), and advanced analytics projects on Azure.

This book is ideal for data engineers and data scientists who want to gain advanced knowledge in Azure Data Factory (a serverless ETL/ELT service on Azure).

© Sudhir Rawat and Abhishek Narain 2019
S. Rawat and A. Narain, *Understanding Azure Data Factory*,
https://doi.org/10.1007/978-1-4842-4122-6_1

What Is Big Data?

Big Data can be defined by following characteristics:

- *Volume*: As the name says, Big Data consists of extremely large datasets that exceed the processing capacity of conventional systems such as Microsoft SQL, Oracle, and so on. Such data is generated through various data sources such as web applications, the Internet of Things (IoT), social media, and line-of-business applications.

- *Variety*: These sources typically send data in a variety of formats such as text, documents (JSON, XML), images, and video.

- *Velocity*: This is the speed at which data is generated is by such sources. High velocity adds to Big Data. For example a factory installed sensor to keep monitor it's temperature to avoid any damage. Such sensors sends E/Sec (event per second) or sometime in millisecond. Generally IoT enable places has many such sensors which sends data so frequently.

- *Veracity*: This is the quality of data captured from various sources. System also generates bias, noise and abnormal data which adds to Big Data. High veracity means more data. It not only adds to big data but also add responsibility to correct it to avoid presenting wrong information to the business user.

Let's think about a fictious retail company called AdventureWorks, which has a customer base across the globe. AdventureWorks has an e-commerce web site and mobile applications for enabling users to shop online, lodge complaints, give feedback, apply for product returns, and so on. To provide the inventory/products to the users, it relies on a business-to-business (B2B) model and partners with vendors (other businesses) that want to list their products on AdventureWorks e-commerce applications. AdventureWorks also has sensors installed on its delivery vans to collect various telemetry data; for example, it provides customers with up-to-date information on consignment delivery and sends alerts to drivers in the case of any issue, for example a high temperature in the delivery van's engine. The company also sends photographers to various trekking sites. All this data is sent back to the company so it can do image classification to understand the gadgets in demand. This helps AdventureWorks stock the relevant items. AdventureWorks also captures feeds from social media in case any feedback/comment/complaint is raised for AdventureWorks.

To get some valuable insights from the huge volume of data, you must choose a distributed and scalable platform that can process the Big Data. Big Data has great potential for changing the way organizations use information to enhance the customer experience, discover patterns in data, and transform their businesses with the insights.

Why Big Data?

Data is the new currency. Data volumes have been increasing drastically over time. Data is being generated from traditional point-of-sale systems, modern e-commerce applications, social sources like Twitter, and IoT sensors/wearables from across the globe. The challenge for any organization today is to analyze this diverse dataset to make more informed decisions that are predictive and holistic rather than reactive and disconnected.

Big Data analytics is not only used by modern organizations to get valuable insights but is also used by organizations having decades-old data, which earlier was too expensive to process, with the availability of pay-as-you-go cloud offerings. As an example, with Microsoft Azure you can easily spin up a 100-node Apache Spark cluster (for Big Data analytics) in less than ten minutes and pay only for the time your job runs on those clusters, offering both cloud scale and cost savings in a Big Data analytics project.

Big Data Analytics on Microsoft Azure

Today practically every business is moving to the cloud because of lucrative reasons such as no up-front costs, infinite scale possibilities, high performance, and so on. The businesses that store sensitive data that can't be moved to the cloud can choose a hybrid approach. The Microsoft cloud (aka Azure) provides three types of services.

- Infrastructure as a service (IaaS)

- Platform as a service (PaaS)

- Software as a service (SaaS)

It seems like every organization on this planet is moving to PaaS. This gives companies more time to think about their business while innovating, improving customer experience, and saving money.

Microsoft Azure offers a wide range of cloud services for data analysis. We can broadly categorize them under storage and compute.

- Azure SQL Data Warehouse, a cloud-based massively parallel-processing-enabled enterprise data warehouse

- Azure Blob Storage, a massively scalable object storage for unstructured data that can be used to search for hidden insights through Big Data analytics

- Azure Data Lake Store, a massively scalable data store (for unstructured, semistructured, and structured data) built to the open HDFS standard

- Azure Data Lake Analytics, a distributed analytics service that makes it easy for Big Data analytics to support programs written in U-SQL, R, Python, and .NET

- Azure Analysis Services, enterprise-grade data modeling tool on Azure (based on SQL Server Analysis Service)

- Azure HDInsight, a fully managed, full-spectrum open source analytics service for enterprises (Hadoop, Spark, Hive, LLAP, Storm, and more)

- Azure Databricks, a Spark-based high-performance analytics platform optimized for Azure

- Azure Machine Learning, an open and elastic AI development tool for finding patterns in existing data and generating models for prediction

- Azure Data Factory, a hybrid and scalable data integration (ETL) service for Big Data and advanced analytics solutions

- Azure Cosmos DB, an elastic and independent scale throughput and storage tool; it also offers throughput, latency, availability, and consistency guarantees with comprehensive service level agreements (SLAs), something no other database service offers at the moment

What Is Azure Data Factory?

Big Data requires a service that can help you orchestrate and operationalize complex processes that in turn refine the enormous structure/semistructured data into actionable business insights.

Azure Data Factory (ADF) is a cloud-based data integration service that acts as the glue in your Big Data or advanced analytics solution, ensuring your complex workflows integrate with the various dependent services required in your solution. It provides a single pane for monitoring all your data movements and complex data processing jobs. Simply said, it is a serverless, managed cloud service that's built for these complex hybrid ETL, ELT, and data integration projects (data integration as a service).

Using Azure Data Factory, you can create and schedule data-driven workflows (called *pipelines*) that can ingest data from disparate data stores. It can process and transform the data by using compute services such as Azure HDInsight Hadoop, Spark, Azure Data Lake Analytics, and Azure Machine Learning (Figure 1-1).

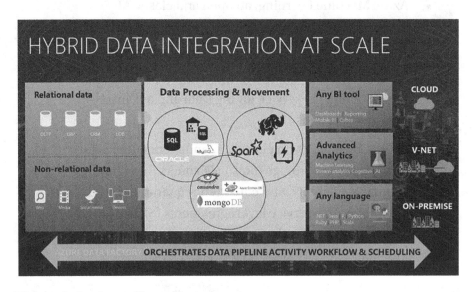

Figure 1-1. *Azure Data Factory*

High-Level ADF Concepts

An Azure subscription might have one or more ADF instances. ADF is composed of four key components, covered in the following sections. These components work together to provide the platform on which you can compose data-driven workflows with steps to move and transform data or execute custom tasks using custom activity that could include deleting files on Azure storage after transforms or simply running additional business logic that is not offered out of the box within Azure Data Factory.

Activity

An *activity* represents an action or the processing step. For example, you copy an activity to copy data between a source and a sink. Similarly, you can have a Databricks notebook activity transform data using Azure Databricks. ADF supports three types of activities: data movement, data transformation, and control flow activities.

Pipeline

A *pipeline* is a logical grouping of activities. Typically, it will contain a set of activities trying to achieve the same end goal. For example, a pipeline can contain a group of activities ingesting data from disparate sources, including on-premise sources, and then running a Hive query on an on-demand HDInsight cluster to join and partition data for further analysis.

The activities in a pipeline can be chained together to operate sequentially, or they can operate independently in parallel.

Datasets

Datasets represent data structures within the data stores, which simply point to or reference the data you want to use in your activities as inputs or outputs.

Linked Service

A *linked service* consists of the connection details either to a data source like a file from Azure Blob Storage or a table from Azure SQL or to a compute service such as HDInsight, Azure Databricks, Azure Data Lake Analytics, and Azure Batch.

Integration Runtime

The *integration runtime* (IR) is the underlying compute infrastructure used by ADF. This is the compute where data movement, activity dispatch, or SSIS package execution happens. It has three different names: Azure, self-hosted, and Azure SQL Server Integration Services (Figure 1-2).

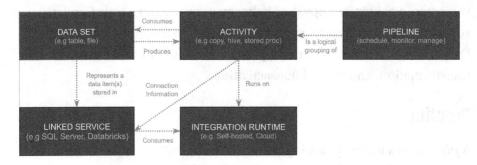

Figure 1-2. *Relationship between ADF components*

When to Use ADF?

The following are examples of when you should use ADF:

- Building a Big Data analytics solution on Microsoft Azure that relies on technologies for handling large numbers of diverse datasets. ADF offers a way to create and run an ADF pipeline in the cloud.

- Building a modern data warehouse solution that relies on technologies such as SQL Server, SQL Server Integration Services (SSIS), or SQL Server Analysis Services (SSAS); see Figure 1-3. ADF provides the ability to run SSIS packages on Azure or build a modern ETL/ELT pipeline letting you access both on-premise and cloud data services.

- Migrating or coping data from a physical server to
  the cloud or from a non-Azure cloud to Azure (blob
  storage, data lake storage, SQL, Cosmos DB). ADF can
  be used to migrate both structured and binary data.

You will learn more about the ADF constructs in Chapter 2.

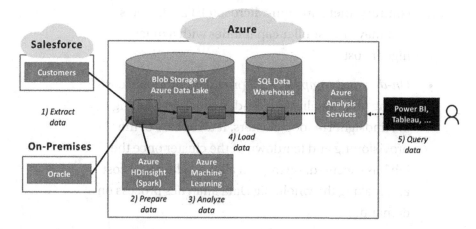

Figure 1-3. *A typical modern data warehouse solution*

Why ADF?

The following are reasons why you should use ADF:

- *Cost effective*: ADF is serverless, and the billing is based
  on factors such as the number of activities run, the data
  movement duration, and the SSIS package execution
  duration. You can find the latest pricing details at
  https://aka.ms/adfpricing.

  For example, if you run your ETL/ ELT pipeline
  hourly, which also involves data movement
  (assuming 100GB data movement per hourly run,
  which should take around 8 minutes with 200MBps

bandwidth), then ADF would bill you not more than $12 for the monthly execution (720 pipeline runs).

Note: The charges for any other service (HDInsight, Azure Data Lake Analytics) are not considered in this calculation. This is solely for the ADF orchestration and data movement cost. On the contrary, there are non-Microsoft ETL/ELT tools that may offer similar capabilities with a much higher cost.

- *On-demand compute*: ADF provides additional cost-saving functionality like on-demand provisioning of Hindsight Hadoop clusters. It takes care of the provisioning and teardown of the cluster once the job has executed, saving you a lot of additional cost and making the whole Big Data analytics process on-demand.

- *Cloud scale*: ADF, being a platform-as-a-service offering, can quickly scale if need be. For the Big Data movement, with data sizes from terabytes to petabytes, you will need the scale of multiple nodes to chunk data in parallel.

- *Enterprise-grade security*: The biggest concern around any data integration solution is the security, as the data may well contain sensitive personally identifiable information (PII).

Since ADF is a Microsoft-owned service (or as I call it a *first-party citizen* on Azure), it follows the same security standards as any other Microsoft service. You can find the security and compliance certification information online.

A common challenge when building cloud applications is to manage the credentials that need to be in your code/ADF pipeline for authenticating to cloud services. Keeping these credentials secure is an important task. Ideally, they never appear on developer workstations or get checked into source control. ADF supports Azure Key Vault, which provides a way to securely store credentials and other keys and secrets, but your code/ADF pipeline needs to authenticate to Key Vault to retrieve them. Managed Service Identity (MSI) makes solving this problem simpler by giving Azure services such as ADF an automatically managed identity in Azure Active Directory (Azure AD). ADF supports MSI and uses this identity to authenticate to any service that supports Azure AD authentication, including Key Vault, without having any credentials in your code/ADF pipeline, which probably is the safest option for service-to-service authentication on Azure.

- *Control flow*: You can chain activities in a sequence, branch based on certain conditions, define parameters at the pipeline level, and pass arguments while invoking the pipeline on-demand or from a trigger. ADF also includes custom state passing and looping containers, that is, for-each iterators.

- *High-performance hybrid connectivity*: ADF supports more than 70 connectors at the time of writing this book. These connectors support on-premise sources as well, which helps you build a data integration solution with your on-premise sources.

- *Easy interaction*: ADF's support for so many connectors makes it easy to interact with all kinds of technologies.

- *Visual UI authoring and monitoring tool*: It makes you super productive as you can use drag-and-drop development. The main goal of the visual tool is to allow you to be productive with ADF by getting pipelines up and running quickly without requiring you to write a single line of code.

- *SSIS package execution*: You can lift and shift an existing SSIS workload.

- *Schedule pipeline execution*: Every business have different latency requirements (hourly, daily, monthly, and so on), and jobs can be scheduled as per the business requirements.

- *Other development options*: In addition to visual authoring, ADF lets you author pipelines using PowerShell, .NER, Python, and REST APIs. This helps independent software vendors (ISVs) build SaaS-based analytics solutions on top of ADF app models.

Summary

Azure Data Factory is a serverless data integration service on the cloud that allows you to create data-driven workflows for orchestrating and automating data movement and data transformation for your advanced analytics solutions. In the upcoming chapters, you will dig deeper into each aspect of ADF with working samples.

CHAPTER 2

Introduction to Azure Data Factory

In any Big Data or advanced analytics solution, the orchestration layer plays an important role in stitching together the heterogenous environments and operationalizing the workflow. Your overall solution may involve moving raw data from disparate sources to a staging/sink store on Azure, running some rich transform jobs (ELT) on the raw data, and finally generating valuable insights to be published using reporting tools and stored in a data warehouse for access. Azure Data Factory is the extract-transform-load (ETL)/extract-load-transform (ELT) service offered by Microsoft Azure.

Azure Data Factory (ADF) is a Microsoft Azure platform-as-a-service (PaaS) offering for data movement and transformation. It supports data movement between many on-premise and cloud data sources. The supported platform list is elaborate and includes both Microsoft and other vendors. It is a powerful tool providing complete flexibility for the movement of structured and unstructured datasets, including RDBMS, XML, JSON, and various NoSQL data stores. Its core strength is the flexibility of being able to use U-SQL or HiveQL.

This chapter will introduce you to Azure Data Factory basics (Figure 2-1). This knowledge will form the building blocks for the advanced analytics solution that you will build later in the book.

© Sudhir Rawat and Abhishek Narain 2019
S. Rawat and A. Narain, *Understanding Azure Data Factory*,
https://doi.org/10.1007/978-1-4842-4122-6_2

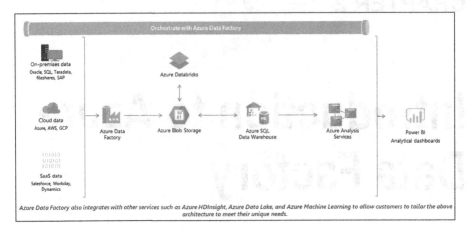

Figure 2-1. *Azure Data Factory basics*

Azure Data Factory v1 vs. Azure Data Factory v2

When you create an Azure Data Factory resource on your Azure subscription, the wizard will ask you to choose between Azure Data Factory v1 and Azure Data Factory v2. Azure Data Factory version 2 is generally available and being actively developed, which means regular feature updates. Azure Data Factory v1 is stabilized, but it's more limited than v2. ADF v2 adds the much needed control flow functionality, which lets data engineers define complex workflows. Monitoring is also an added enhancement in v2, making it much richer and natively integrating it with Azure Monitor and Microsoft Operations Management Suite for building single-pane-of-glass monitoring. One of the biggest features of v2 is the integration of SQL Server Integration Services (SSIS). Many Microsoft customers have been using SSIS for their data movement needs primarily involving SQL Server databases for many years because SSIS has been in existence for a long time. The integration of SSIS and Azure Data Factory has been a key customer requirement for migrating to the PaaS platform for ETL without needing to rewrite the entire data transformation logic across the enterprise.

The recent release of Azure Data Factory v2 has taken a major step toward meeting this requirement. SSIS packages can now be integrated with ADF and can be scheduled/orchestrated using ADF v2. The SSIS package execution capability makes all fine-grained transformation capabilities and SSIS connectors available from within ADF. Customers can utilize existing ETL assets while expanding ETL capabilities with the ADF platform.

ADF v2 allows SSIS packages to be moved to the cloud using the integration runtime (IR) to execute, manage, monitor, and deploy these packages to Azure. The IR allows for three different scenarios: Azure (a pure PaaS with endpoints), self-hosted (within a private network), and Azure-SSIS (a combination of the two).

The capability of SSIS package integration with ADF has led to the expansion of a core feature of the ADF platform. Specifically, there is now a separate control flow in the ADF platform. The activities are broken into data transformation activities and control flow activities; this is similar to the SSIS platform.

In addition to the SSIS integration, ADF v2 has expanded its functionality on a few other fronts. It now supports an extended library of expressions and functions that can be used in the JSON string value. Data pipeline monitoring is available using OMS tools in addition to the Azure portal. This is a big step toward meeting the requirements of customers with established OMS tools for any data movement activity.

There has also been a change in job scheduling in ADF v2. In the prior version, jobs were scheduled based on time slices. This feature has been expanded in ADF v2. Jobs can be scheduled based on triggering events, such as the completion of a data refresh in the source data store.

In this book, we will focus on Azure Data Factory v2, but most of the features are applicable to v1 too.

Data Integration with Azure Data Factory

Azure Data Factory offers a code-free, drag-and-drop, visual user interface to maximize productivity by getting data pipelines up and running quickly. You can also connect the visual tool directly to your Git repository for a seamless deployment workflow. Using Azure Data Factory, you can create and schedule data-driven workflows (called *pipelines*) that can ingest data from disparate data stores. ADF can process and transform the data by using compute services such as Azure HDInsight Hadoop, Spark, Azure Data Lake Analytics, Azure Cosmos DB, and Azure Machine Learning.

You can also write your own code in Python, .NET, the REST API, Azure PowerShell, and Azure Resource Manager (ARM) to build data pipelines using your existing skills. You can choose any compute or processing service available on Azure and put them into managed data pipelines to get the best of both the worlds.

Architecture

When you create an Azure Data Factory v2 resource on your Azure subscription, you create a data integration account. This is sort of a serverless workplace where you can author your data pipelines. You are not billed for this step. You pay for what you use, and that will happen only when you execute some pipeline.

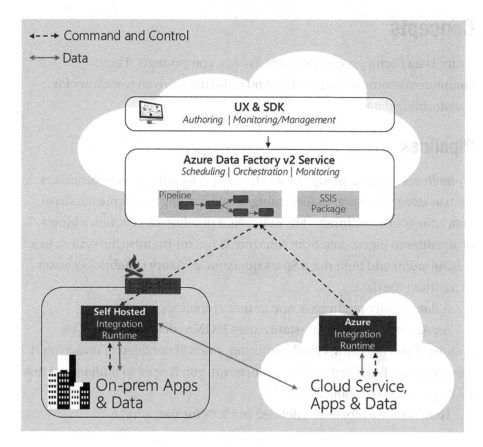

Figure 2-2. *ADF architecture showing the command/ control flow versus data flow during orchestration*

Once you start authoring the pipeline, the ADF service stores the pipeline metadata in the selected ADF region. When your pipeline is executed, the orchestration logic runs on some compute, in other words, the integration runtime. There are three types of IR used for different purposes, and I will talk about the use of each one of them in the upcoming sections.

Concepts

Azure Data Factory is composed of five key components. These components come together while you build data-driven workflows for transforming data.

Pipelines

A *pipeline* is a logical grouping of activities performing a set of processes such as extracting data, transforming it, and loading into some database, data warehouse, or storage. For example, a pipeline can contain a group of activities to ingest data from Amazon S3 (an on-premise file system to a staging store) and then run a Spark query on an Azure Databricks cluster to partition the data.

A data factory might have one or more pipelines.

An Azure Data Factory instance uses JSON to describe each of its entities. If you are using visual authoring, you will not need to understand this structure. But when writing code/script, you'll need to understand this JSON payload (see Table 2-1).

Here is how a pipeline is defined in JSON format:

```
{
    "name": "PipelineName",
    "properties":
    {
        "description": "pipeline description",
        "activities":
        [
        ],
        "parameters": {
          }
    }
}
```

Table 2-1. *Pipeline Properties*

Tag	Description	Type	Required
name	Specifies the name of the pipeline. Use a name that represents the action that the pipeline performs. Maximum number of characters: 140. Must start with a letter, number, or underscore (_). The following characters are not allowed: . + ? / < > * % & : \	String	Yes
description	Specifies the text describing what the pipeline is used for.	String	No
activities	The pipeline can have one or more activities defined within it.	Array	Yes
parameters	The parameters property can have one or more parameters defined within the pipeline, making your pipeline flexible for reuse.	List	No

Activities

Activities represent a processing step in a pipeline. These are specific tasks that compose the overall pipeline. For example, you might use a Spark activity, which runs a Spark query against Azure Databricks or an HDInsight cluster, to transform or analyze your data. Azure Data Factory supports three types of activities: data movement (copy activities), data transform (compute activities), and control activities.

Execution Activities (Copy and Data Transform)

The following are the execution activities:

- Copy supports 70+ connectors for copying data from the source to the sink, including binary copy. I will cover this in depth in Chapter 3.

- Data transform supports the transform activities in Table 2-2.

Table 2-2. *Transform Activities*

Data Transformation Activity	Compute Environment
Hive	HDInsight (Hadoop)
Pig	HDInsight (Hadoop)
MapReduce	HDInsight (Hadoop)
Hadoop streaming	HDInsight (Hadoop)
Spark	HDInsight (Hadoop)
Machine learning activities: batch execution and update resource	Azure VM
Stored procedure	Azure SQL, Azure SQL Data Warehouse, or SQL Server
U-SQL	Azure Data Lake Analytics
Cosmos DB	Azure Cosmos DB
Custom code	Azure Batch
Databricks notebook	Azure Databricks
Databricks JAR	Azure Databricks
Databricks Python	Azure Databricks

You will learn more about transform activities in Chapter 4.

Here is some sample JSON of an execution activity:

```
{
    "name": "Execution Activity Name",
    "description": "description",
    "type": "<ActivityType>",
    "typeProperties":
    {
    },
    "linkedServiceName": "MyLinkedService",
    "policy":
    {
    },
    "dependsOn":
    {
    }
}
```

Table 2-3 describes the properties in the activity JSON definition.

Table 2-3. *Activity Properties*

Property	Description	Required
name	Name of the activity. Specify a name that represents the action that the activity performs.	Yes
description	Text describing what the activity is or is used for.	Yes
type	Type of the activity. Different types of activities include data movement, data transformation, and control activities.	Yes

(*continued*)

Table 2-3. (*continued*)

Property	Description	Required
linkedServiceName	Name of the linked service used by the activity. An activity may require that you specify the linked service that links to the required compute environment.	Yes for HDInsight Activity, Azure Machine Learning, Batch Scoring Activity, and Stored Procedure Activity No for all others
typeProperties	Properties in the typeProperties section depend on each type of activity.	No
policy	Policies that affect the runtime behavior of the activity. This property includes timeout and retry behavior. If it is not specified, default values are used. For more information, see the "Activity "Policy" section.	No
dependsOn	Defines activity dependencies and how subsequent activities depend on previous activities. For more information, see the "Activity Dependency" section.	No

Activity Policy

You can configure the runtime behavior of an activity by enforcing various policies onto it. Table 2-4 shows the properties.

Here is an activity policy JSON definition:

```json
{
    "name": "MyPipelineName",
    "properties": {
      "activities": [
        {
          "name": "MyCopyBlobtoSqlActivity"
          "type": "Copy",
          "typeProperties": {
            ...
          },
          "policy": {
            "timeout": "00:10:00",
            "retry": 1,
            "retryIntervalInSeconds": 60,
            "secureOutput": true
          }
        }
      ],
        "parameters": {
          ...
        }
    }
}
```

Table 2-4. *Activity Properties*

JSON Name	Description	Allowed Values	Required
timeout	Specifies the timeout for the activity to run.	Timespan	No. Default timeout is 7 days.
retry	Specifies the maximum retry attempts.	Integer	No. Default is 0.
retryInterval InSeconds	Specifies the delay between retry attempts in seconds.	Integer	No. Default is 20 seconds.
secureOutput	When set to true, output from the activity is considered as secure and will not be logged to monitoring.	Boolean	No. Default is false.

Control

Table 2-5 describes the control activities.

Table 2-5. *Control Activities*

Name	Description
Execute Pipeline	The Execute Pipeline activity allows an Azure Data Factory pipeline to invoke another pipeline.
ForEach	The ForEach activity defines a repeating control flow in your pipeline. This activity is used to iterate over a collection and executes specified activities in a loop. The loop implementation of this activity is similar to a ForEach looping structure in programming languages.
Web	The Web activity can be used to call a custom REST endpoint from an Azure Data Factory pipeline. You can pass datasets and linked services to be consumed and accessed by the activity.
Lookup	The Lookup activity can be used to read or look up a record/table name/value from any external source. This output can further be referenced by succeeding activities.
Get Metadata	The Get Metadata activity can be used to retrieve the metadata of any data in Azure Data Factory.
Until	This activity implements a Do-Until loop that is similar to a Do-Until looping structure in programming languages. It executes a set of activities in a loop until the condition associated with the activity evaluates to true. You can specify a timeout value for the Until activity in Azure Data Factory.

(continued)

Table 2-5. (*continued*)

Name	Description
If Condition	The If Condition activity can be used to branch based on a condition that evaluates to true or false. The If Condition activity provides the same functionality that an `if` statement provides in programming languages. It evaluates a set of activities when the condition evaluates to true and another set of activities when the condition evaluates to false.
Wait	When you use a Wait activity in a pipeline, the pipeline waits for the specified period of time before continuing with the execution of subsequent activities.

Control activities have the following top-level structure (see Table 2-6):

```
{
    "name": "Control Activity Name",
    "description": "description",
    "type": "<ActivityType>",
    "typeProperties":
    {
    },
    "dependsOn":
    {
    }
}
```

Table 2-6. *Control activity properties*

Property	Description	Required
name	This specifies the name of the activity. Specify a name that represents the action that the activity performs. Maximum number of characters: 55. Must start with a letter, a number, or an underscore (_). Following characters are not allowed: . + ? / < > * % & : \	Yes
description	This specifies the text describing what the activity or is used for.	Yes
type	This specifies the type of the activity. Different types of activities include data movement, data transformation, and control activities.	Yes
typeProperties	Properties in the typeProperties section depend on each type of activity.	No
dependsOn	This property is used to define the activity dependency and how subsequent activities depend on previous activities.	No

Activity Dependency

You can create a dependency between two activities in ADF. This is extremely helpful while you want to run downstream activities on certain conditions or dependencies. ADF lets you build the dependencies based on various conditions such as Succeeded, Failed, Skipped, and Completed.

For example, when Activity A is successfully executed, then run Activity B. If Activity A fails, then run Activity C. Activity B depends on Activity A succeeding.

```
{
    "name": "PipelineName",
    "properties":
    {
        "description": "pipeline description",
        "activities": [
         {
            "name": "MyFirstActivity",
            "type": "Copy",
            "typeProperties": {
            },
            "linkedServiceName": {
            }
        },
        {
            "name": "MySecondActivity",
            "type": "Copy",
            "typeProperties": {
            },
            "linkedServiceName": {
            },
            "dependsOn": [
            {
                "activity": "MyFirstActivity",
                "dependencyConditions": [
                    "Succeeded"
                ]
            }
```

```
        ]
      }
    ],
    "parameters": {
      }
    }
  }
}
```

Datasets

A *dataset* is the representation or reference to the actual data in the data store. For a data movement activity like a Copy activity, you can set a source and a sink dataset accordingly for the data movement.

For example, to copy data from Azure Blob Storage to a SQL database, you create two linked services: Azure Blob Storage and Azure SQL Database. Then, create two datasets: an Azure Blob dataset (which refers to the Azure Storage linked service) and an Azure SQL table dataset (which refers to the Azure SQL Database linked service). The Azure Storage and Azure SQL Database linked services contain connection strings that Azure Data Factory uses at runtime to connect to your Azure storage and Azure SQL database, respectively. The Azure Blob dataset specifies the blob container and blob folder that contains the input blobs in your Blob Storage. The Azure SQL table dataset specifies the SQL table in your SQL database to which the data is to be copied.

Here is a dataset JSON example:

```
{
    "name": "<name of dataset>",
    "properties": {
        "type": "<type of dataset: AzureBlob, AzureSql etc...>",
        "linkedServiceName": {
                "referenceName": "<name of linked service>",
```

```
                "type": "LinkedServiceReference",
        },
        "structure": [
            {
                "name": "<Name of the column>",
                "type": "<Name of the type>"
            }
        ],
        "typeProperties": {
            "<type specific property>": "<value>",
            "<type specific property 2>": "<value 2>",
        }
    }
}
```

Table 2-7 describes the properties in the previous JSON listing.

Table 2-7. *Properties*

Property	Description	Required
name	This specifies the name of the dataset. It has the same naming rules as the Azure Data Factory instance name.	Yes
type	This specifies the type of the dataset. Specify one of the types supported by the Azure Data Factory instance (for example, AzureBlob, AzureSqlTable).	Yes
structure	This specifies the schema of the dataset. For details, see "Dataset Structure."	No
typeProperties	The type properties are different for each type (for example, AzureBlob, AzureSqlTable). For details on the supported types and their properties, see "Dataset Type."	Yes

Dataset Structure

This is optional. It defines the schema of the dataset by containing a collection of names and data types of columns. You use the `structure` section to provide type information that is used to convert types and map columns from the source to the destination.

Each column in the structure contains the properties in Table 2-8.

Table 2-8. Dataset Properties

Property	Description	Required
name	Name of the column.	Yes
type	Data type of the column. Azure Data Factory supports the following interim data types as allowed values: Int16, Int32, Int64, Single, Double, Decimal, Byte[], Boolean, String, Guid, Datetime, Datetimeoffset, and Timespan.	No
culture	.NET-based culture to be used when the type is a .NET type: Datetime or Datetimeoffset. The default is en-us.	No
format	Format string to be used when the type is a .NET type: Datetime or Datetimeoffset.	No

Here's an example of a Blob dataset.

```
"structure":
[
    { "name": "userid", "type": "Int64"},
    { "name": "name", "type": "String"},
    { "name": "lastlogindate", "type": "Datetime", "culture":
    "fr-fr", "format": "ddd-MM-YYYY"}
]
```

When to Specify a Dataset Structure?

When you are copying data within strong schema-based relational stores and want to map source columns to sink columns and their names are not the same, you can specify a dataset structure.

You may also specify a dataset structure when your source contains no schema or a weak schema like text files in Blob Storage, which needs to be converted to native types in sink during the Copy activity.

Linked Services

Linked services are like connection strings that define the connectivity information that Azure Data Factory needs to connect to the respective external data stores or compute engines. A linked service defines the connection information, while the dataset represents the actual structure of the data. For example, an Azure Storage linked service specifies a connection string/SAS URI to connect to the Azure storage account. Additionally, an Azure blob dataset specifies the blob container and the folder that contains the data.

Linked services are used for two purposes in Azure Data Factory.

- To represent a data store that includes but isn't limited to an on-premises SQL Server database, Oracle database, file share, or Azure blob storage account.

- To represent a compute resource that can host the execution of an activity. For example, the Databricks Jar activity runs on an HDInsight Hadoop cluster.

Figure 2-3 shows the relationship between the linked service, dataset, activity, pipeline, and integration runtime.

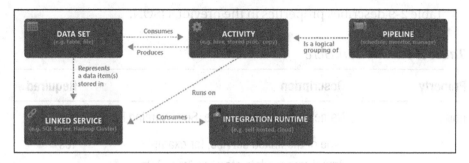

Figure 2-3. *Relationship between Azure Data Factory components*

Linked Service Example

The following linked service is an Azure Storage linked service. Notice that
the type is set to AzureStorage. The type properties for the Azure Storage
linked service include a connection string. The Azure Data Factory service
uses this connection string to connect to the data store at runtime.

```
{
    "name": "AzureStorageLinkedService",
    "properties": {
        "type": "AzureStorage",
        "typeProperties": {
            "connectionString": {
                "type": "SecureString",
                "value": "DefaultEndpointsProtocol=https;Account
                Name=<accountname>;AccountKey=<accountkey>"
            }
        },
        "connectVia": {
            "referenceName": "<name of Integration Runtime>",
            "type": "IntegrationRuntimeReference"
        }
    }
}
```

Table 2-9 describes properties in the previous JSON.

Table 2-9. *Caption Here*

Property	Description	Required
name	Name of the linked service. See "Naming Rules."	Yes
type	Type of the linked service, for example AzureStorage (data store) or AzureBatch (compute). See the description for typeProperties.	Yes
typeProperties	The type properties are different for each data store or compute.	Yes
connectVia	The IR to be used to connect to the data store. You can use the Azure IR or self-hosted IR (if your data store is in a private network). If not specified, it uses the default Azure IR.	No

Integration Runtime

The integration runtime (IR) is the compute infrastructure used by Azure Data Factory to provide the following data integration capabilities across different network environments:

- *Data movement*: Move data between data stores in public networks and data stores in private networks (on-premise or virtual private networks). It provides support for built-in connectors, format conversion, column mapping, and performant and scalable data transfer. It applies to the Azure IR and self-hosted IR.

- *Data transform activity dispatch*: Dispatch and monitor transformation activities running on a variety of compute services such as Azure HDInsight, Azure Machine Learning, Azure SQL Database, SQL Server, and more. It applies to the Azure IR and self-hosted IR.

- *SSIS package execution*: Natively execute SQL Server Integration Services packages in a managed Azure compute environment. It applies to the Azure-SSIS IR.

In Azure Data Factory, an activity defines the action to be performed. A linked service defines a target data store or a compute service. An integration runtime provides the bridge between the activity and the linked services. It is referenced by the linked service and provides the compute environment where the activity either runs or gets dispatched from. This way, the activity can be performed in the region closest possible to the target data store or compute service in the most performant way while meeting security and compliance needs.

Azure Data Factory offers three types of IR, and you should choose the type that best serves the data integration capabilities and network environment you are looking for. These three types are covered next.

Azure IR

The Azure integration runtime can be used for data movement and orchestration of data stores and compute services that are in the public network. For example, if you're copying data from public endpoints like Amazon S3 to Azure Blob in a public environment, then the Azure IR works well and provide you with cloud scale for big data movement as shown in Figure 2-4.

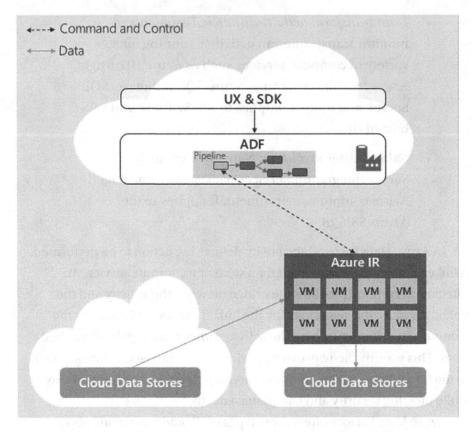

Figure 2-4. *Azure integration runtime scalability (cloud to cloud scenario)*

The Azure IR is a fully managed integration runtime. It is completely serverless and supports cloud scale. You don't have to worry about infrastructure provision, software installation, patching, or capacity scaling. In addition, you pay only for the duration of the actual utilization. You can set how many data integration units to use on the Copy activity, and the compute size of the Azure IR is elastically scaled up accordingly without you having to explicitly adjust the size of the Azure IR.

The only drawback of the Azure IR is it cannot be used if your data stores are behind a firewall because then it would require inbound access through the firewall, which may not be agreeable.

By default, each data factory has an Azure IR in the back end that supports operations on cloud data stores and compute services in public networks. The location of that Azure IR is auto-resolved. If the `connectVia` property is not specified in the linked service definition, the default Azure IR is used. You need to explicitly create an Azure IR only when you would like to explicitly define the location of the IR or when you would like to virtually group the activity executions on different IRs for management purposes.

You can specify the location of the Azure IR, in which case the data movement and activity dispatch will happen in that specific region. Azure IR is available in almost all Azure regions.

Being able to specify the Azure IR location is handy in scenarios where strict data compliance is required and you need to ensure that the data do not leave a certain geography. For example, if you want to copy data from Azure Blob in Southeast Asia to SQL Azure in Southeast Asia and want to ensure data never leaves the Southeast Asia region, then create an Azure IR in Southeast Asia and link both the linked services to this IR.

If you choose to use the auto-resolve Azure IR, which is the default option, during the Copy activity ADF will make a best effort to automatically detect your sink and source data store to choose the best location either in the same region or in the closest region. During the Lookup/GetMetadata and Transform activities, ADF will use the IR in the data factory region.

For the Copy activity, ADF will make a best effort to automatically detect your sink and source data store to choose the best location either in the same region if available or in the closest one in the same geography, or if not detectable to use the data factory region as an alternative.

For Lookup/GetMetadata activity execution and transformation activity dispatching, ADF will use the IR in the data factory region.

Self-Hosted IR

The self-hosted IR can be used while doing hybrid data integration. If you want to perform data integration securely in a private network, which does not have a direct line of sight from the public cloud environment, you can install a self-hosted IR in an on-premise environment behind your corporate firewall or inside an Azure virtual network (Figure 2-5).

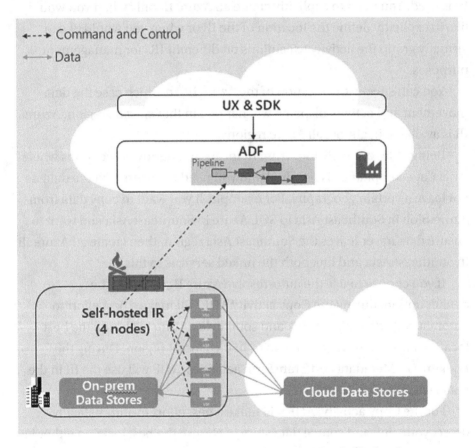

Figure 2-5. *Self-hosted IR inside corporate network (hybrid scenario)*

The self-hosted integration runtime is not serverless and needs to be manually installed on a Windows machine. It does support high availability and can be installed on up to four machines. The self-hosted integration runtime only makes outbound HTTP-based connections to the open Internet. It can also be used to orchestrate transform activities inside an Azure virtual network. For example, if you must execute a stored procedure on an on-premise SQL Server or orchestrate jobs on HDInsight clusters inside a virtual network with NSGs (Network Security Group) enabled, you should use a self-hosted integration which has a line of sight to the on-premise SQL Server or HDInsight clusters inside the virtual network.

From a security perspective, a self-hosted IR stores all the credentials/secrets that are part of the linked services in Azure Data Factory locally, and the values are encrypted using the Windows DPAPI. This way, the on-premise credentials never leave the security boundary of the enterprise.

To compare the self-hosted IR with the Azure IR, the self-hosted IR is not serverless and needs to be managed by you. The cost of orchestrating activities on the self-hosted IR is minuscule, but you still must bring your own infrastructure. The self-hosted integration runtime supports transparent auto-update features, and once you set up the infrastructure on which it runs, the auto-update happens by itself typically once a month. Auto-update is an important feature as the Azure Data Factory team keeps improving the software on a monthly release cycle. The improvements may include support for new connectors, bug fixes, security patches, and performance improvements.

When you move the data between on-premises and cloud, the Copy activity uses a self-hosted integration runtime to transfer the data from the on-premise data source to the cloud and vice versa.

While authoring a linked service, you can choose a self-hosted integration runtime by specifying the `connectvia` property. By doing so, you are ensuring the secrets/connection strings in the linked service are stored on the self-hosted integration runtime.

While using UI, the credentials are encrypted using the JavaScript Cryptography library and sent to the self-hosted IR where they are decrypted and encrypted again using the Windows DPAPI. An encrypted linked service is sent back to the ADF service for storing the linked service reference.

You can use PowerShell locally to encrypt the credentials directly against a self-hosted integration runtime and can send the encrypted payload back to the ADF service for storing the linked service reference. I would consider this as the securest option for setting linked service credentials in the self-hosted IR.

While using REST or an SDK, the linked service payload goes securely through the ADF service to the self-hosted IR, on which it is encrypted and stored, and a reference is sent back to ADF.

The self-hosted IR is logically registered to the Azure Data Factory instance, and the compute used to support its functionalities is provided by you. Therefore, there is no explicit location property for the self-hosted IR. If you have provisioned an Azure virtual network and would like to do the data integration inside the virtual network, you can set up the self-hosted IR on a Windows virtual network inside a virtual network.

When used to perform data movement, the self-hosted IR extracts data from the source and writes into the destination.

Azure-SSIS IR

The Azure-SSIS IR can run an existing SSIS package in the cloud. It can be provisioned in either a public network or a virtual private network. Since the Azure-SSIS IR only runs the package, it should have a line of sight to source and sink databases. If it needs to access a database that is on-premises, then you can join the Azure-SSIS IR to your on-premise network using a site-to-site VPN or ExpressRoute private peering.

The Azure-SSIS IR is a fully managed cluster of Azure VMs dedicated to run your SSIS packages. You can bring your own Azure SQL database or managed instance server to host the catalog of SSIS projects/packages (SSISDB) that will be attached to it. You can scale up the power of the compute by specifying the node size and scale it out by specifying the number of nodes in the cluster. You can manage the cost of running your Azure-SSIS integration runtime by stopping and starting it as you see fit.

For more information, see Chapter 7, which covers the creation and configuration of the Azure-SSIS IR. Once it's created, you can deploy and manage your existing SSIS packages with little to no change using familiar tools such as SQL Server Data Tools (SSDT) and SQL Server Management Studio (SSMS), just like using SSIS on-premises.

Selecting the right location for your Azure-SSIS IR is essential to achieving high performance in your ETL workflows.

The location of your Azure-SSIS IR does not need be the same as the location of your Azure Data Factory instance, but it should be the same as the location of your own Azure SQL database/managed instance server where SSISDB is to be hosted. This way, your Azure-SSIS integration runtime can easily access SSISDB without incurring excessive traffic between different locations.

If you do not have an existing Azure SQL database/managed instance (preview) server to host SSISDB but you have on-premises data sources/destinations, you should create a new Azure SQL database/managed instance (preview) server in the same location of a virtual network connected to your on-premises network. This way, you can create your Azure-SSIS IR using the new Azure SQL database/managed instance (preview) server and joining that virtual network, all in the same location, effectively minimizing data movement across different locations.

If the location of your existing Azure SQL database/managed instance (preview) server where SSISDB is hosted is not the same as the location of a virtual network connected to your on-premise network, first create your

Azure-SSIS IR using an existing Azure SQL database/managed instance (preview) server and joining another virtual network in the same location and then configure a virtual network to a virtual network connection between different locations.

Hands-on: Creating a Data Factory Instance Using a User Interface

We will create an Azure Data Factory (version 2) instance in the following steps:

Prerequisites

These are the prerequisites:

- An Azure subscription with the contributor role assigned to at least one resource group

- A web browser (Chrome/Microsoft Edge)

Steps

Here are the steps:

1. Navigate to the Azure portal within your web browser and navigate to `https://portal.azure.com` (see Figure 2-6).

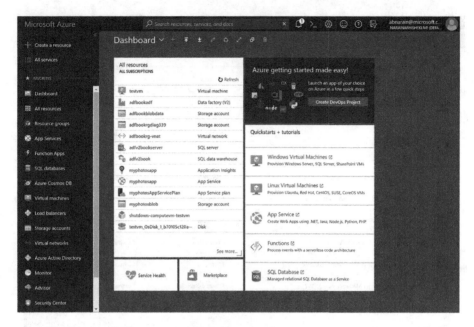

Figure 2-6. *Azure portal*

2. Click the "Resource groups" icon in the left menu.

3. Click "+Add" and create a new resource group. Let's call it adf-rg, and select South East Asia as the region.

4. After a few seconds, click the Refresh button and select the new resource group.

5. Click +Add and search for d*ata factory* in the search box (Figure 2-7).

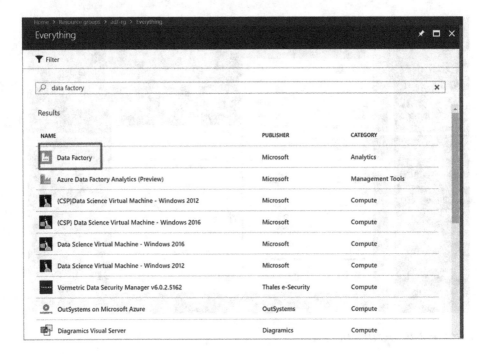

Figure 2-7. *Data Factory in Azure Portal*

6. Select Data Factory, and click Create (see Figure 2-8).

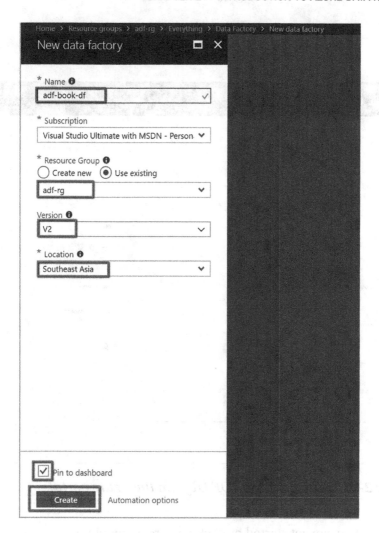

Figure 2-8. *Creating a Data Factory v2 instance*

Note   The Data Factory instance name is globally unique, so you may not be able to use the same name as shown here. Please append some string to adf-book-df to keep the name unique.

---

7.   Once it is created, click Author & Monitor to log into the ADF UI (Figure 2-9).

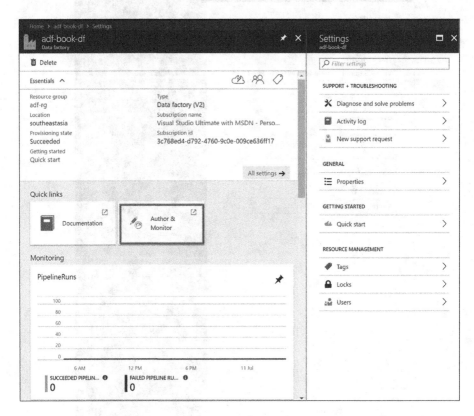

Figure 2-9. *Launching the ADF UI from the Azure portal*

8.   You can get started by clicking "Create pipeline" (Figure 2-10).

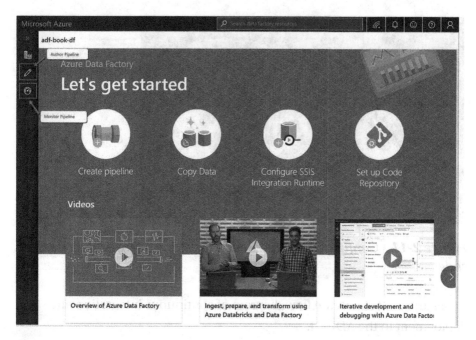

Figure 2-10. *ADF user interface for authoring and monitoring data pipelines*

Let's cover some ADF UI features. Setting up a code repository is extremely useful for the continuous integration/continuous deployment (CI/CD) of your data pipelines (see Figure 2-11). In a team, each data engineer can work on their branches and merge/commit their changes to the master branch, which will be published into production. All the source code generated by the ADF UI can be configured to be stored in Visual Studio Teams Services and GitHub.

Figure 2-11. *Configuring a code repository for storing ADF-generated code*

Figure 2-12 shows the flow diagram of continuous integration and deployment in the ADF UI.

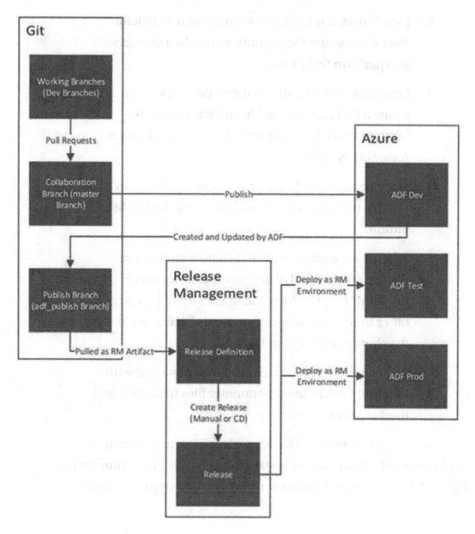

Figure 2-12. *CI/CD workflow in ADF*

Here are the steps:

1. Set up a development ADF instance with VSTS/
   GitHub where all developers can author ADF
   resources such as pipelines, datasets, and more.

2. Developers can modify resources such as pipelines. They can use the Debug button to debug changes and perform test runs.

3. Once satisfied with the changes, developers can create a PR (pull request) from their branch to master or collaboration branch to get the changes reviewed by peers.

4. Once changes are in the master branch, they can publish to the development ADF using the Publish button.

5. When your team is ready to promote changes to the test and prod ADF instances, you can export the ARM template from the master branch or any other branch in case your master is behind the live development ADF instance.

6. The exported ARM template can be deployed with different environment parameter files to the test and prod environments.

You can also set up a VSTS release definition to automate the deployment of a Data Factory instance to multiple environments (see Figure 2-13). Get more information and detailed steps in Chapter 9.

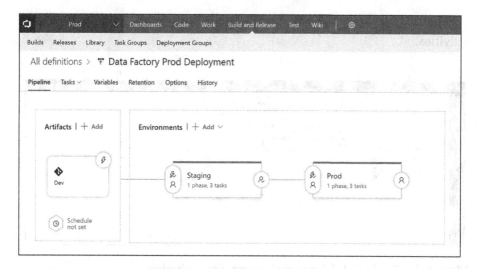

Figure 2-13. *VSTS release definition*

Figure 2-14 shows the process of using author pipelines via drag-and-drop development.

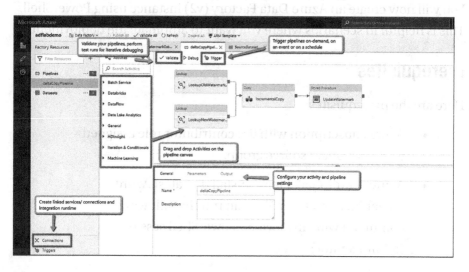

Figure 2-14. *ADF UI for authoring*

Figure 2-15 shows the process of visually monitoring pipelines/ activities.

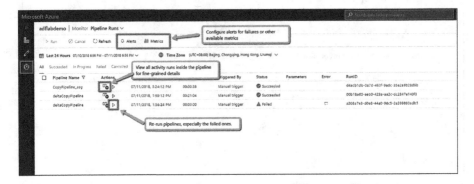

Figure 2-15. *ADF UI for monitoring data pipelines*

Hands-on: Creating a Data Factory Instance Using PowerShell

You will now create an Azure Data Factory (v2) instance using PowerShell. This is helpful in scenarios where you want to automate the deployments.

Prerequisites

Here are the prerequisites:

- Azure subscription with the contributor role assigned to at least one resource group.

- Azure PowerShell. Please install the latest Azure PowerShell modules. You can run the following command with an elevated PowerShell session (administrator):

```
#If not installed already
Install-Module -Name AzureRM
```

```
#To update existing Azure PowerShell module
Update-Module -Name AzureRM
```

- Web browser (Chrome/Microsoft Edge).

Log In to PowerShell

Follow these steps:

1. Launch PowerShell on your machine. Keep PowerShell open until the end of this example. If you close and reopen it, you will need to run these commands again.

2. Run the following command, and enter the same Azure username and password that you used to sign in to the Azure portal:

   ```
   Connect-AzureRmAccount
   ```

3. Run the following command to view all the subscriptions for this account:

   ```
   Get-AzureRmSubscription
   ```

4. If you see multiple subscriptions associated with your account, run the following command to select the subscription that you want to work with. Replace SubscriptionId with the ID of your Azure subscription:

   ```
   Select-AzureRmSubscription -SubscriptionId
   "<SubscriptionId>"
   ```

Create a Data Factory

Run this code:

```
Set-AzureRmDataFactoryV2 -ResourceGroupName rgname -Location
eastus -Name adflabdemo
```

Notes:

- If the resource group/Data Factory instance name already exists, you may want to try a new name.

- To create Data Factory instances, the user account you use to log in to Azure must be a member of the contributor or owner roles or an administrator of the Azure subscription.

- Please make sure Data Factory is available in the region specified in the previous cmdlet.

Summary

In this chapter, you successfully created an Azure Data Factory instance and went through high-level constructs of the PaaS ETL/ELT service.

A fictitious company was briefly discussed in Chapter 1; we will continue to describe this scenario and current pain points. AdventureWorks is a retail company that requires assistance in managing and finding insight on the data received on a regular interval. Currently, the company has data available from various sources.

These are the challenges the company is facing:

- *Data volume*: Since day 1 AdventureWorks has had data available in different sources and different formats. Handling such a huge amount of data is becoming challenging for the company.

- *No single version of the truth*: There are multiple versions of each analysis, which makes it hard to believe in any data output. Most of the employees' time is spent figuring out whether the output data is the right one or not.

- *Many data input points*: Over a period of time many data input points have been introduced. The company provides a mobile app to the consumer for shopping and provides various channels to capture feedback, capture data from social media, and connect various vendors to find various data patterns.

- *No automation*: Currently, there are manual steps involved in various stages that affect the latency, data quality, and cost. The company wants to automate the entire process, from getting the raw data, transforming it, and making it available for business users to take some actions on it.

- *Security*: This is a topmost concern of the AdventureWorks company. The managers always worry about data security. Many processes, tools, and human involvement makes the company invest many resources to make sure the data is secure.

- *High latency*: Now you are getting a sense of the various processes involved that impact in latency. Every organization wants the right information to be available at the right time.

- *Cost*: The cost involves infrastructure, maintenance, support, various process, and so on. The company wants to know how the costs can be reduced.

As you notice, the company spends most of its time solving issues that impact the day-to-day business.

The job is to help AdventureWorks set up an end-to-end solution on Azure that will help the company overcome these concerns. Figure 2-16 shows the architecture you'll build on in upcoming chapters that will help AdventureWorks focus more on business innovation.

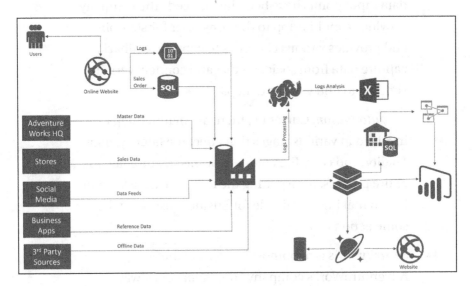

Figure 2-16. *Sample architecture*

CHAPTER 3

Data Movement

Any extract-transform-load (ETL) or extract-load-transform (ELT) project
starts with data ingestion (Figure 3-1). You should be able to connect
to various sources, either in a public network or behind firewalls in a
private network, and then be able to pull them onto a staging location or
a destination on the cloud. In the ELT pattern for Big Data processing, you
would generally dump all your data in a staging blob or data lake on the
cloud, and based on the need, you would run analytical jobs/transform
activities to get further insights or even do some basic data cleansing.

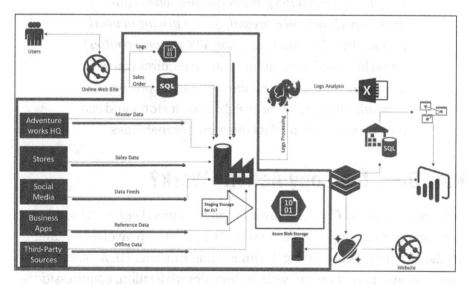

Figure 3-1. *Extraction of data from disparate sources during ETL/ELT*

© Sudhir Rawat and Abhishek Narain 2019
S. Rawat and A. Narain, *Understanding Azure Data Factory*,
https://doi.org/10.1007/978-1-4842-4122-6_3

This chapter will focus on building the data extraction pipelines for AdventureWorks.

Overview

In ADF, the Copy activity is used to extract the data from various sources. The Copy activity is executed at an integration runtime. You need to select the right integration runtime for your copy jobs.

- *Use the Azure integration runtime when your source and sink are publicly accessible.* You need to understand that even though the Azure integration runtime provides you with a serverless infrastructure for data movement, it runs in a public Azure environment. This means the Azure integration runtime needs a line of sight to your data stores.

- *Use the self-hosted integration runtime when either of the sources is behind a firewall or in a private network (Azure virtual network, Amazon VPC, or on-premises).* The self-hosted integration runtime requires you to install software on a machine in the same private network, which has line of sight to your stores and can provide you with the data integration capabilities.

How Does the Copy Activity Work?

Let's try to break the Copy activity into smaller units (Figure 3-2) to understand what happens in each step. The initial step involves reading the data from the source using the integration runtime. Then, based on the copy configuration, there are serialization/deserialization, compression/decompression, and column mapping, format conversion, and so on, taking place. The final step is to write this data into the sink/destination.

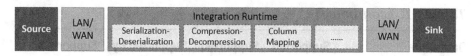

Figure 3-2. *Classification of the Copy activity timeline*

Supported Connectors

At the time of writing this book, ADF supports more than 70 connectors, and more are being added all the time (Table 3-1).

Table 3-1. *Connectors*

Data Store	Supported Source	Supported Sink	Supported by the Azure IR	Supported by the Self-Hosted IR
Azure Blob Storage	✓	✓	✓	✓
Azure Cosmos DB	✓	✓	✓	✓
Azure Data Lake Storage Generation 1	✓	✓	✓	✓
Azure Data Lake Storage Generation 2 (Preview)	✓	✓	✓	✓
Azure Database for MySQL	✓		✓	✓
Azure Database for PostgreSQL	✓		✓	✓
Azure File Storage	✓	✓	✓	✓
Azure SQL Database	✓	✓	✓	✓
Azure SQL Data Warehouse	✓	✓	✓	✓

(*continued*)

Table 3-1. (*continued*)

Data Store	Supported Source	Supported Sink	Supported by the Azure IR	Supported by the Self-Hosted IR
Azure Search Index		✓	✓	✓
Azure Table Storage	✓	✓	✓	✓
Amazon Redshift	✓		✓	✓
DB2	✓		✓	✓
Drill (Preview)	✓		✓	✓
Google BigQuery	✓		✓	✓
Greenplum	✓		✓	✓
HBase	✓		✓	✓
Hive	✓		✓	✓
Apache Impala (Preview)	✓		✓	✓
Informix	✓			✓
MariaDB	✓		✓	✓
Microsoft Access	✓			✓
MySQL	✓			✓
Netezza	✓		✓	✓
Oracle	✓	✓	✓	✓
Phoenix	✓		✓	✓
PostgreSQL	✓			✓
Presto (Preview)	✓		✓	✓

(*continued*)

Table 3-1. (*continued*)

Data Store	Supported Source	Supported Sink	Supported by the Azure IR	Supported by the Self-Hosted IR
SAP Business Warehouse	✓			✓
SAP HANA	✓	✓		✓
Spark	✓		✓	✓
SQL Server	✓	✓	✓	✓
Sybase	✓			✓
Teradata	✓			✓
Vertica	✓		✓	✓
Cassandra	✓		✓	✓
Couchbase (Preview)	✓		✓	✓
MongoDB	✓		✓	✓
Amazon S3	✓		✓	✓
File System	✓	✓	✓	✓
FTP	✓		✓	✓
HDFS	✓		✓	✓
SFTP	✓		✓	✓
Generic HTTP	✓		✓	✓
Generic OData	✓		✓	✓
Generic ODBC	✓	✓		✓
Amazon Marketplace Web Service (Preview)	✓		✓	✓

(*continued*)

Table 3-1. (*continued*)

Data Store	Supported Source	Supported Sink	Supported by the Azure IR	Supported by the Self-Hosted IR
Common Data Service for Apps	✓	✓	✓	✓
Concur (Preview)	✓		✓	✓
Dynamics 365	✓	✓	✓	✓
Dynamics CRM	✓	✓	✓	✓
GE Historian	✓			✓
HubSpot (Preview)	✓		✓	✓
Jira (Preview)	✓		✓	✓
Magento (Preview)	✓		✓	✓
Marketo (Preview)	✓		✓	✓
Oracle Eloqua (Preview)	✓		✓	✓
Oracle Responsys (Preview)	✓		✓	✓
PayPal (Preview)	✓		✓	✓
QuickBooks (Preview)	✓		✓	✓
Salesforce	✓	✓	✓	✓
Salesforce Service Cloud	✓	✓	✓	✓
Salesforce Marketing Cloud (Preview)	✓		✓	✓

(*continued*)

Table 3-1. (*continued*)

Data Store	Supported Source	Supported Sink	Supported by the Azure IR	Supported by the Self-Hosted IR
SAP Cloud for Customer (C4C)	✓	✓	✓	✓
SAP ECC	✓		✓	✓
ServiceNow	✓		✓	✓
Shopify (Preview)	✓		✓	✓
Square (Preview)	✓		✓	✓
Web Table (HTML table)	✓			✓
Xero (Preview)	✓		✓	✓
Zoho (Preview)	✓		✓	✓

The connectors that are marked as previews are still in development. You can still use them and even provide feedback to Microsoft. If required, feel free to contact Microsoft Support to get information regarding the preview connectors.

We recommend you refer to the ADF documentation for the latest list of supported connectors. You can check http://bit.ly/adfconnectors or simply scan the QR code in Figure 3-3.

Figure 3-3. *QR code pointing to connector documentation in ADF*

Configurations

Let's now discuss the Copy activity.

Supported File and Compression Formats

Let's get into the details of how a copy works. When you choose to copy a file or a folder with multiple files, you need to specify whether ADF should treat it as a binary file and copy it as is or whether you want to perform some lightweight transforms on it, in which case it will not be treated as a binary file.

- If you specify a binary copy while configuring the Copy activity, then ADF copies it as is, without modifying any of its content. You may still choose to rename it in the destination/sink if need be. As it may seem, this approach is efficient in copying large datasets as there is no serialization/deserialization, and so on, involved in this approach. If you are migrating something like petabyte-scale data to the cloud, it is best to copy it as is (binary copy).

- When you do not specify a binary copy in the Copy activity configuration, then you can utilize various lightweight transforms in ADF like format conversion between text, JSON, Avro, ORC, and Praquet. You

can also read or write compressed files using the
supported compression codecs: GZip, Deflate, BZip2,
and ZipDeflate. In this approach, ADF parses the
file content and performs the format conversion/
compression as desired.

Copy Activity Properties

Before we get into the hands-on steps, let's take a quick look at some
sample JSON:

```
"activities":[
    {
        "name": "CopyActivityTemplate",
        "type": "Copy",
        "inputs": [
            {
                "referenceName": "<source dataset name>",
                "type": "DatasetReference"
            }
        ],
        "outputs": [
            {
                "referenceName": "<sink dataset name>",
                "type": "DatasetReference"
            }
        ],
        "typeProperties": {
            "source": {
                "type": "<source type>",
                <properties>
            },
```

```
            "sink": {
                "type": "<sink type>"
                <properties>
            },
            "translator":
            {
                "type": "TabularTranslator",
                "columnMappings": "<column mapping>"
            },
            "dataIntegrationUnits": <number>,
            "parallelCopies": <number>,
            "enableStaging": true/false,
            "stagingSettings": {
                <properties>
            },
            "enableSkipIncompatibleRow": true/false,
            "redirectIncompatibleRowSettings": {
                <properties>
            }
        }
    }
]
```

The above JSON template of a Copy activity contains an exhaustive list of supported properties. You can use the ones that are required. While using the ADF UI, these properties will be autogenerated. Table 3-2 shows the list shows the property descriptions.

Property Details

Table 3-2 shows the property details.

Table 3-2. *Properties*

Property	Description	Required
type	The type property of a Copy activity must be set to Copy.	Yes
inputs	Specify the dataset you created that points to the source data. The Copy activity supports only a single input.	Yes
outputs	Specify the dataset you created that points to the sink data. The Copy activity supports only a single output.	Yes
typeProperties	Specify a group of properties to configure the Copy activity.	Yes
source	Specify the copy source type and the corresponding properties on how to retrieve data. Please check the Microsoft documentation for each connector to find the latest supported source properties.	Yes
sink	Specify the copy sink type and the corresponding properties for how to write data. Please check the Microsoft documentation for each connector to find the latest supported sink properties.	Yes
translator	Specify explicit column mappings from the source to the sink. This applies when the default copy behavior cannot fulfill your needs.	No

(continued)

Table 3-2. (*continued*)

Property	Description	Required
data IntegrationUnits	Specify the powerfulness of the Azure integration runtime to empower the data copy. This was formerly known as cloud data movement units (DMUs).	No
parallelCopies	Specify the parallelism that you want the Copy activity to use when reading data from the source and writing data to the sink.	No
enableStaging staging Settings	Choose to stage the interim data in blob storage instead of directly copying data from the source to the sink.	No
enableSkip IncompatibleRowre directIncompatibleRow Settings	Choose how to handle incompatible rows when copying data from the source to the sink.	No

How to Create a Copy Activity

You can create a Copy activity using visual authoring (ADF UI). Once you have created an Azure Data Factory instance, you can directly navigate to https://adf.azure.com.

Within the ADF UI, you can either choose the Copy Data tool or author a Copy activity by dragging it into the authoring canvas (Figure 3-4).

Figure 3-4. *Authoring canvas*

The Copy Data tool (Table 3-3) simplifies the data ingestion process by optimizing the experience for a first-time data-loading experience. It hides many ADF details and properties that may not be useful while doing basic job such as loading data into the data lake.

Table 3-3. *Copy Data Tool*

Copy Data Tool	Per Activity (Copy Activity) Authoring Canvas
You want to easily build a data-loading task without learning about Azure Data Factory entities (linked services, datasets, pipelines, etc.).	You want to implement complex and flexible logic for loading data into a lake.
You want to quickly load a large number of data artifacts into a data lake.	You want to chain the Copy activity with subsequent activities for cleansing or processing data.

Schema Capture and Automatic Mapping in Copy Data Tool

The schema of a data source may not be the same as the schema of a data destination in many cases. In this scenario, you need to map columns from the source schema to columns from the destination schema.

The Copy Data tool monitors and learns your behavior when you are mapping columns between source and destination stores. After you pick one or a few columns from the source data store and map them to the destination schema, the Copy Data tool starts to analyze the pattern for column pairs you picked from both sides. Then, it applies the same pattern to the rest of the columns. Therefore, you will see that all the columns have been mapped to the destination in the way you want after just a few clicks. If you are not satisfied with the choice of column mapping provided by the Copy Data tool, you can ignore it and continue manually mapping the columns. Meanwhile, the Copy Data tool constantly learns and updates the pattern and ultimately reaches the right pattern for the column mapping you want to achieve.

When copying data from SQL Server or Azure SQL Database into Azure SQL Data Warehouse, if the table does not exist in the destination store, the Copy Data tool supports the creation of the table automatically by using the source schema.

Technically, both of them will end up creating the following:

- Linked services for the source data store and the sink data store.

- Datasets for the source and the sink.

- A pipeline with a Copy activity. The next section provides an example.

Scenario: Creating a Copy Activity Using the Copy Data Tool (Binary Copy)

Go to https://adf.azure.com (a prerequisite is to already have an Azure Data Factory instance created). We will copy data from Amazon S3 to Azure Blob Storage.

Click the Copy Data icon (see Figure 3-5).

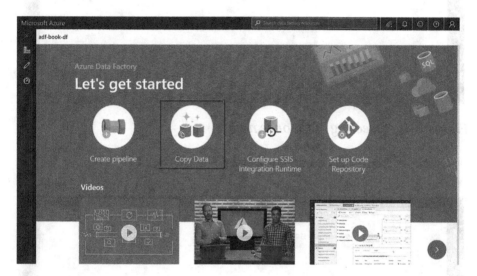

Figure 3-5. *Copy Data icon*

You will see a dialog for configuring the Copy activity. The task name will become the pipeline name. You can provide a description for your reference.

You can specify a task schedule, which defines a cadence for this copy workflow. This is useful in the case of incremental data-loading scenarios. For now, click "Run once now" and then click Next (see Figure 3-6).

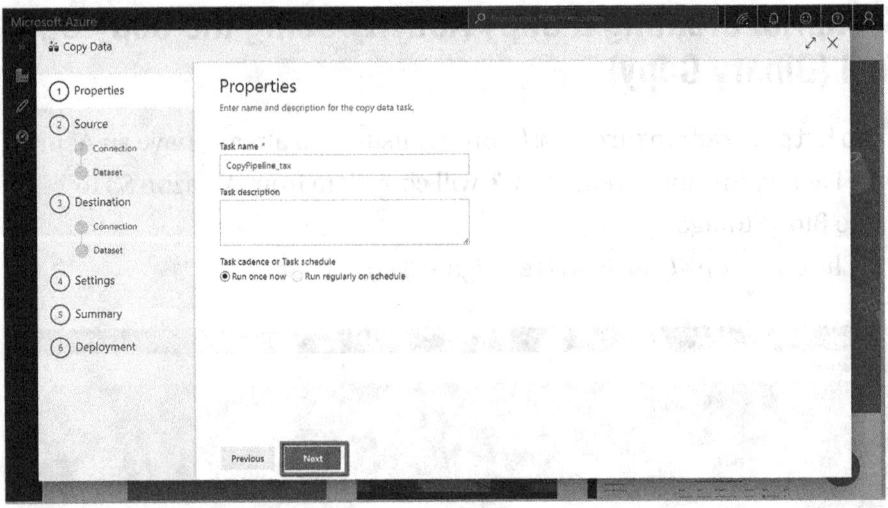

Figure 3-6. *Selecting "Run once now"*

Click "+ Create new connection" (see Figure 3-7).

Figure 3-7. *Creating a new connection*

The next dialog lets you select the new linked service (connection to source). In Figure 3-8, we are connecting to Amazon S3 as the source. You may use your desired connector.

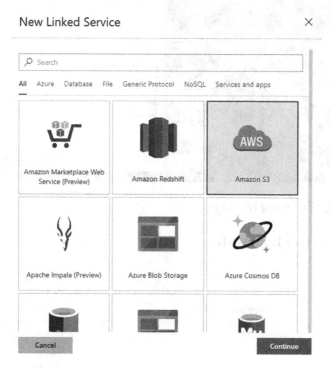

Figure 3-8. *Connecting to Amazon S3*

Enter the access key ID and secret access key. You can validate the credentials by selecting the test connection (see Figure 3-9). Click Finish.

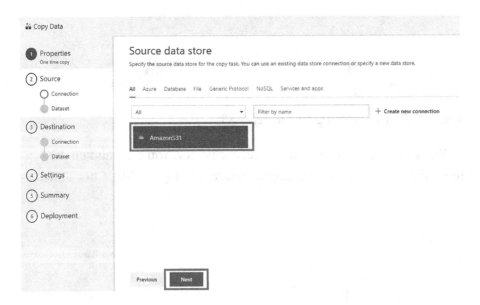

Figure 3-9. *Entering the keys*

Click Next (see Figure 3-10).

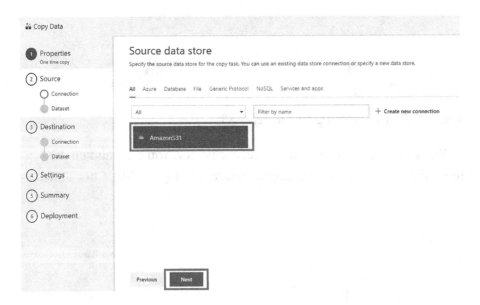

Figure 3-10. *Select the source data store. Clicking Next*

In the dialog, you can configure the dataset. You can select the correct file or folder to copy data from (see Figure 3-11). You can navigate to the folders by clicking Browse. We will use binary copy. You can also select the compression in this step. In this example, we are not using compression. Enabling compression will have some performance degradation as it is a resource-intensive operation.

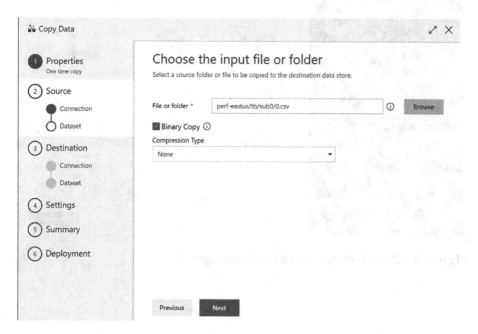

Figure 3-11. *Selecting the folder*

Click Next.

Create a destination linked service. Select Azure Blob Storage. Click
Continue (see Figure 3-12).

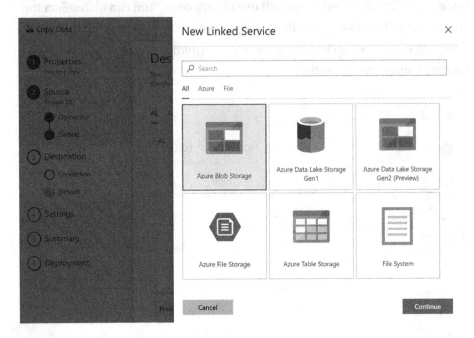

Figure 3-12. *Selecting Azure Blob Storage*

Add the connection details (see Figure 3-13). Click Finish.

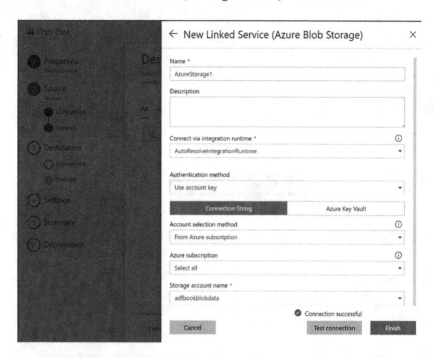

Figure 3-13. *Adding the connection details*

Click Next (see Figure 3-14).

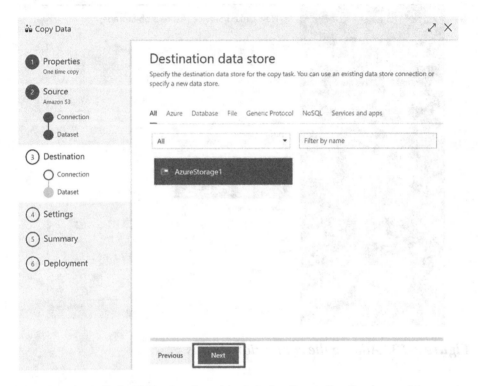

Figure 3-14. *Select the destination/ sink where the data would be copied. Clicking Next*

Choose the folder path in the destination (see Figure 3-15). This is where the data will be copied into.

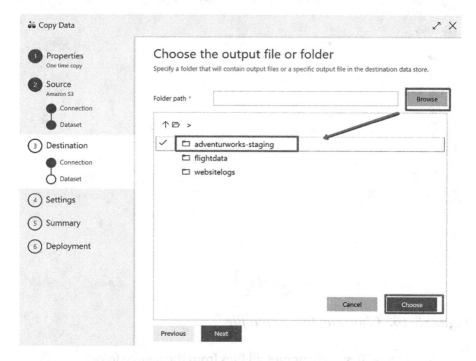

Figure 3-15. *Setting the destination*

Click Next. In addition to the compression, you can see a copy behavior property (see Figure 3-16), which is a specific property related to the Blob Storage dataset when it is a sink. The following are the allowed values:

- *PreserveHierarchy (default)*: This preserves the file hierarchy in the target folder. The relative path of the source file to the source folder is identical to the relative path of the target file to the target folder.

- *FlattenHierarchy*: All files from the source folder are in the first level of the target folder. The target files have autogenerated names.

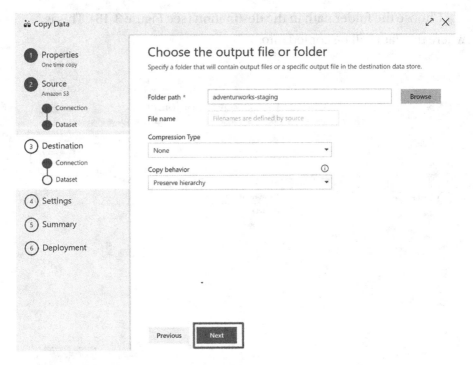

Figure 3-16. *Choosing the output file*

> – *MergeFiles*: This merges all files from the source folder
> to one file. If the file or blob name is specified, the
> merged file name is the specified name. Otherwise, it's
> an autogenerated file name.

Click Next.

Click Next (see Figure 3-17).

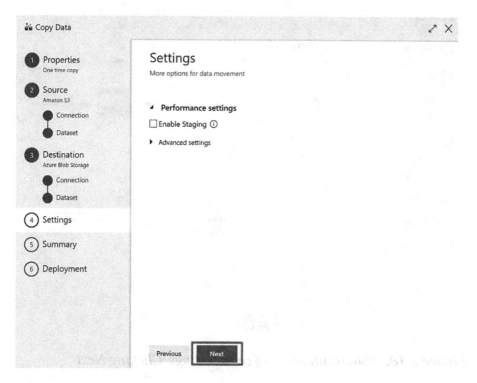

Figure 3-17. *Configuring settings*

Click Next (see Figure 3-18).

Figure 3-18. *Shows summary of copy settings. Clicking Next*

Click Monitor to monitor the pipeline run (see Figure 3-19).

Figure 3-19. *You can find copy status in the monitoring section to track the progress of the copy activity. Clicking Monitor*

Under monitoring you will see the status of the pipelines. Under Actions, select View Activity Runs as highlighted in red (see Figure 3-20).

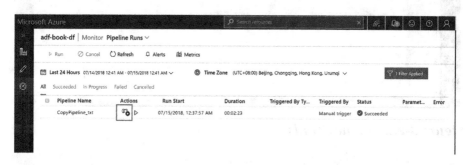

Figure 3-20. *Status*

Click the view the details as highlighted in red (see Figure 3-21).

Figure 3-21. *Details*

You can find all the monitoring details, including data volume and throughput (see Figure 3-22).

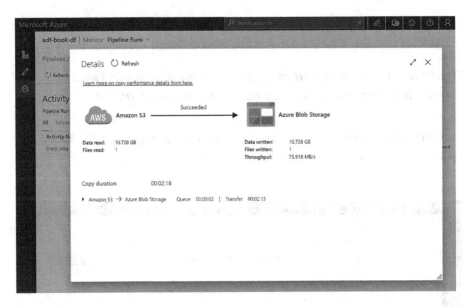

Figure 3-22. *All the details*

Copy Performance Considerations

Microsoft has published a reference for performance during the Copy activity. This is a great indicator to help you understand if you are getting the optimum performance.

Figure 3-23 shows the copy throughput number in MBps for the given source and sink pairs in a single Copy activity run based on in-house testing. For comparison, it also demonstrates how different settings of data integration units or self-hosted integration runtime scalability (multiple nodes) can help on copy performance.

	(Unit: MBps)	# of cloud DMUs OR gateway nodes	Cloud Sinks: Azure Blob (GRS)	Cloud Sinks: Azure Data Lake Storage Gen1	Cloud Sinks: Azure Data Lake Storage Gen2	Cloud Sinks: Azure SQL Data Warehouse (6000 DWU): PolyBase	Cloud Sinks: Azure SQL Data Warehouse (6000 DWU): Bulk Insert	Cloud Sinks: Azure SQL Database (P11)	Cloud Sinks: Azure Cosmos DB (SQL API; 100,000 RU)	Cloud Sinks: Azure Table	On-prem Sinks**: On-prem SQL Server	On-prem Sinks**: On-prem File System
Cloud Sources	Azure Blob (GRS)	4	56	56	56	1250	*	5	6	*	11	129
		8	**105**	**105**	**105**		*	9	12	0.2		
	Azure Data Lake Storage Gen1	4	56	56	56	1060	*	5	6	*	10	114
		8	**120**	**108**	**120**		*	9	12	*		
	Azure Data Lake Storage Gen2	4	56	56	56	*	*	5	6	*	11	130
		8	**120**	**108**	**120**		*	9	12	*		
	Azure SQL Data Warehouse (2000 DWU)	4	9	8	9	6	1	8	6	0.3	11	*
	Azure SQL Database (P11)	4	9	8	9	6	1	8	6	0.3	14	*
	Azure Table	4	2	2	2	*	2	2	1	1	1	*
	Azure Cosmos DB (SQL API; 100,000 RU)	4	2	2	2	*	2	2	2	*	*	*
	Amazon S3	8	**107**	**101**	**120**	69	*	*	*	*	*	*
	Amazon Redshift	4	*	*	*	7.2	*	*	*	*	*	*
On-prem Sources	On-premises SQL Server	1	7	7	7	18	0.4	7	6	0.2	*	*
	On-premises File System	1	195	192	*	102	0.3	6	6	0.2	*	*
		4	**505**	**510**	*	*					*	*
	On-premise HDFS	1	179	183	*	83	0.3	3	6	0.2	*	*
		4	**500**	**525**	*	*					*	*

Unit: MBps

**: The throughput numbers for this source-sink combination will be published later.*

***: For copying from cloud sources to on-prem sinks, single Self-hosted Integration Runtime node was used.*

Figure 3-23. *Copy throughput numbers*

Data Integration Units

A *data integration unit* (DIU), formerly known as *cloud data movement unit* (DMU), is a measure that represents the power (a combination of CPU, memory, and network resource allocation) of a single unit in Azure Data Factory. A DIU applies only to the Azure integration runtime and not to the self-hosted integration runtime.

The minimal DIUs to empower the Copy activity run is two. If none is specified, the default is used. Table 3-4 lists the default DIUs used in different copy scenarios:

Table 3-4. *Default DIUs*

Copy Scenario	Default DIUs Determined by Service
Copy data between file-based stores	Between 4 and 32, depending on the number and size of the files
All other copy scenarios	4

To override the defaults, specify a value for the `dataIntegrationUnits` property. The allowed values for the `dataIntegrationUnits` property is up to 256. The actual number of DIUs that the copy operation uses at runtime is equal to or less than the configured value, depending on your data pattern.

You can easily find the DIU units used through the ADF UI monitoring during a Copy activity that uses the Azure integration runtime.

DIUs are what you get charged for; hence, this has a direct billing implication.

Parallel Copy

You can use the `parallelCopies` property to indicate the parallelism that you want the Copy activity to use. You can think of this property as the maximum number of threads within the Copy activity that can read from your source or write to your sink data stores in parallel.

For each Copy activity run, Azure Data Factory determines the number of parallel copies to use to copy data from the source data store and to the destination data store. The default number of parallel copies that it uses depends on the type of source and sink you are using (Table 3-5).

Table 3-5. *Copy Scenarios*

Copy Scenario	Default Parallel Copy Count Determined by Service
Copy data between file-based stores	Depends on the size of the files and the number of DIUs used to copy data between two cloud data stores, or the physical configuration of the self-hosted integration runtime machine
Copy data from any source data store to Azure Table Storage	4
All other copy scenarios	1

While copying data across file-based stores, the `parallelCopies` property determines the parallelism at the file level. The chunking within a single file will happen underneath automatically and transparently, and it's designed to use the best suitable chunk size for a given source data store type to load data in parallel and orthogonal to `parallelCopies`. The actual number of parallel copies the data movement service uses for the copy operation at runtime is no more than the number of files you have. If the copy behavior is `mergeFile`, the Copy activity cannot take advantage of file-level parallelism.

When you specify a value for the `parallelCopies` property, consider the load increase on your source and sink data stores and to the self-hosted integration runtime if the copy activity is empowered by it, for example, for hybrid copy. This happens especially when you have multiple activities or concurrent runs of the same activities that run against the same data store. If you notice that either the data store or the self-hosted integration runtime is overwhelmed with the load, decrease the `parallelCopies` value to relieve the load.

When you copy data from stores that are not file-based to stores that are file-based, the data movement service ignores the `parallelCopies` property. Even if parallelism is specified, it's not applied in this case.

`parallelCopies` is orthogonal to `dataIntegrationUnits`. The former is counted across all the DIUs.

Staged Copy

When you copy data from a source data store to a sink data store, you might choose to use Blob Storage as an interim staging store. Staging is especially useful in the following cases:

- You want to ingest data from various data stores into a SQL data warehouse via PolyBase. A SQL data warehouse uses PolyBase as a high-throughput mechanism to load a large amount of data into a SQL data warehouse. However, the source data must be in Blob Storage or Azure Data Lake Store, and it must meet additional criteria. When you load data from a data store other than Blob Storage or Azure Data Lake Store, you can activate data copying via interim staging Blob Storage. In that case, Azure Data Factory performs the required data transformations to ensure that it meets the requirements of PolyBase. Then it uses PolyBase to load data into the SQL data warehouse efficiently.

- Sometimes it takes a while to perform a hybrid data movement (that is, to copy from an on-premises data store to a cloud data store) over a slow network connection. To improve performance, you can use a staged copy to compress the data on-premises so that it takes less time to move data to the staging data store in the cloud and then to decompress the data in the staging store before loading into the destination data store.

- You don't want to open ports other than port 80 and port 443 in your firewall because of corporate IT policies. For example, when you copy data from an on-premises data store to an Azure SQL Database sink or an Azure SQL Data Warehouse sink, you need to activate outbound TCP communications on port 1433 for both the Windows firewall and your corporate firewall. In this scenario, the staged copy can take advantage of the self-hosted integration runtime to first copy data to a Blob Storage staging instance over HTTP or HTTPS on port 443 and then load the data into SQL Database or SQL Data Warehouse from Blob Storage staging. In this flow, you don't need to enable port 1433.

How Staged Copy Works

When you activate the staging feature, first the data is copied from the source data store to the staging Blob Storage (bring your own). Next, the data is copied from the staging data store to the sink data store. Azure Data Factory automatically manages the two-stage flow for you. Azure Data Factory also cleans up temporary data from the staging storage after the data movement is complete.

When you run copy activity using a staging store, you can specify whether you want the data to be compressed before moving data from the source data store to an interim or staging data store and then to be decompressed before moving data from an interim or staging data store to the sink data store. This is helpful in scenarios where you are ingesting data from low intenet bandwidth network, as the compressed data would require lower bandwidth which later is decompressed on cloud (staging storage).

Currently, you can't copy data between two on-premises data stores by using a staging store.

Configuration

Configure the enableStaging setting in the Copy activity to specify whether you want the data to be staged in Blob Storage before you load it into a destination data store. When you set enableStaging to TRUE, specify the additional properties listed in Table 3-6. If you don't specify one, you also need to create an Azure storage or storage shared access signature-linked service for staging.

Table 3-6. *Configuration Details*

Property	Description	Default Value	Required
enableStaging	Specify whether you want to copy data via an interim staging store.	False	No
linkedServiceName	Specify the name of an AzureStorage linked service, which refers to the instance of storage that you use as an interim staging store. You cannot use storage with a shared access signature to load data into SQL Data Warehouse via PolyBase. You can use it in all other scenarios.	N/A	Yes, when enableStagingis is set to TRUE

(continued)

90

Table 3-6. (*continued*)

Property	Description	Default Value	Required
path	Specify the Blob Storage path that you want to contain the staged data. If you do not provide a path, the service creates a container to store temporary data. Specify a path only if you use storage with a shared access signature or you require temporary data to be in a specific location.	N/A	No
enableCompression	Specifies whether data should be compressed before it is copied to the destination. This setting reduces the volume of data being transferred.	False	No

Here's a sample definition of the Copy activity with the properties that are described in the preceding table:

```
"activities":[
    {
        "name": "Sample copy activity",
        "type": "Copy",
        "inputs": [...],
```

```
        "outputs": [...],
        "typeProperties": {
            "source": {
                "type": "SqlSource",
            },
            "sink": {
                "type": "SqlSink"
            },
            "enableStaging": true,
            "stagingSettings": {
                "linkedServiceName": {
                    "referenceName": "MyStagingBlob",
                    "type": "LinkedServiceReference"
                },
                "path": "stagingcontainer/path",
                "enableCompression": true
            }
        }
    }
}
]
```

Staged Copy Billing Impact

You are charged based on two steps: copy duration and copy type.

When you use staging during a cloud copy (copying data from a cloud data store to another cloud data store, with both stages empowered by Azure integration runtime), you are charged as follows:

[sum of copy duration for step 1 and step 2] x [cloud copy unit price]

When you use staging during a hybrid copy (copying data from an on-premises data store to a cloud data store, with one stage empowered by the self-hosted integration runtime), you are charged for the following:

[hybrid copy duration] x [hybrid copy unit price] + [cloud copy duration] x [cloud copy unit price]

Considerations for the Self-Hosted Integration Runtime

If your Copy activity is executed on a self-hosted integration runtime, note the following:

Setup: Microsoft recommends that you use a dedicated machine to host the integration runtime. The recommended configuration for the self-hosted integration runtime machine is at least 2GHz, four cores, 8GB RAM, and 80GB disk.

Scale out: A single logical self-hosted integration runtime with one or more nodes can serve multiple Copy activity runs at the same time concurrently. If you have a heavy need on hybrid data movement, either with a large number of concurrent Copy activity runs or with a large volume of data to copy, consider scaling out the self-hosted integration runtime so as to provision more resources to empower the copy.

Considerations for Serialization and Deserialization

Serialization and deserialization can occur when your input dataset or output dataset is a file.

The copy behavior is to copy files between file-based data stores.

When input and output data sets both have the same or no file format settings, the data movement service executes a binary copy without any serialization or deserialization. You will see a higher throughput compared to the scenario where the source and sink file format settings are different from each other.

When input and output datasets both are in text format and only the encoding type is different, the data movement service does only encoding conversion. It doesn't do any serialization and deserialization, which causes some performance overhead compared to a binary copy.

When the input and output datasets both have different file formats or different configurations, like delimiters, the data movement service deserializes the source data to the stream, transforms it, and then serializes it into the output format you indicated. This operation results in more significant performance overhead compared to other scenarios.

When you copy files to/from a data store that is not file-based (for example, from a file-based store to a relational store), the serialization or deserialization step is required. This step results in significant performance overhead.

The file format you choose might affect copy performance. For example, Avro is a compact binary format that stores metadata with data. It has broad support in the Hadoop ecosystem for processing and querying. However, Avro is more expensive for serialization and deserialization, which results in lower copy throughput compared to text format. Make your choice of file format throughout the processing flow holistically.

Considerations for Compression

When your input or output data set is a file, you can set the Copy activity to perform compression or decompression as it writes data to the destination. When you choose compression, you make a trade-off between input/output (I/O) and CPU. Compressing the data costs extra in compute resources. But in return, it reduces network I/O and storage. Depending on your data, you may see a boost in overall copy throughput.

- *Codec*: Each compression codec has advantages. For example, BZip2 has the lowest copy throughput, but you get the best Hive query performance with BZip2 because you can split it for processing. Gzip is the most balanced option, and it is used the most often. Choose the codec that best suits your end-to-end scenario.

- *Level*: You can choose from two options for each compression codec: fastest compressed and optimally compressed. The fastest compressed option compresses the data as quickly as possible, even if the resulting file is not optimally compressed. The optimally compressed option spends more time on compression and yields a minimal amount of data. You can test both options to see which provides better overall performance in your case.

To copy a large amount of data between an on-premises store and the cloud, consider using a staged copy with compression enabled. Using interim storage is helpful when the bandwidth of your corporate network and your Azure services is the limiting factor, and you want both the input data set and output data set to be in uncompressed form.

Considerations for Column Mapping

You can set the `columnMappings` property in the Copy activity to map all or a subset of the input columns to the output columns. After the data movement service reads the data from the source, it needs to perform column mapping on the data before it writes the data to the sink. This extra processing reduces copy throughput.

If your source data store is queryable, for example, if it's a relational store like SQL database or SQL Server, or if it's a NoSQL store like Azure Table Storage or Azure Cosmos DB, consider pushing the column filtering and reordering logic to the query property instead of using column mapping. This way, the projection occurs while the data movement service reads data from the source data store, where it is much more efficient.

Summary

It is extremely important to understand the performance bottlenecks before operationalizing your data pipelines. In this chapter, you focused on the data movement aspect that comprises the extract phase of ETL.

CHAPTER 4

Data Transformation: Part 1

What is the purpose of data if there are no insights derived from it? Data transformation is an important process that helps every organization to get insight and make better business decisions. This chapter you will focus on why data transformation is important and how Azure Data Factory helps in building this pipeline.

Data Transformation

Now days many organizations have tons of data coming from disparate data sources, and at times it's unclear to the company what can be done with this data. The data is generally scattered across various sources such as SQL Server, Excel, business applications, and so on. You might even find people who have data in a file that they frequently refer to. At the end of the day, not only do you want to bring all the data together, but you also want to transform it to get insight from it. The insight reflects how the company did in the past and how they are doing in the present and future as well. Let's say a company has 10 to 20 years of data. These are the kinds of questions that can be answered after data transformation: How many sales were there in a specific period? What regions had the most sales? How many sales are expected in the future?

© Sudhir Rawat and Abhishek Narain 2019
S. Rawat and A. Narain, *Understanding Azure Data Factory*,
https://doi.org/10.1007/978-1-4842-4122-6_4

Azure Data Factory provides various compute options to perform data transformation. Let's get started with each service to understand how they work and what their benefits are. This will make them easier to understand when you use these services through Azure Data Factory.

HDInsight

Microsoft HDInsight (also known as Hadoop on Azure) is a Big Data processing framework available as a service. This means companies do not have to bother setting up a big cluster to process data. This is important; otherwise, it takes a minimum of three months to procure hardware, install the operating system and software, configure machines, apply security, and design for scalability, fault tolerance, and support and maintenance. Microsoft HDInsight provides users with the ability to spin up a cluster in minutes. It takes care of all the features such as security, scalability, and others behind the scenes. This will allow organizations to save money and focus more on solving business problems and innovating in their solutions.

HDInsight doesn't use HDFS on the cluster for storage; instead, it uses Azure Blob Storage or Azure Data Lake Store to store data. Figure 4-1 shows a typical HDInsight architecture.

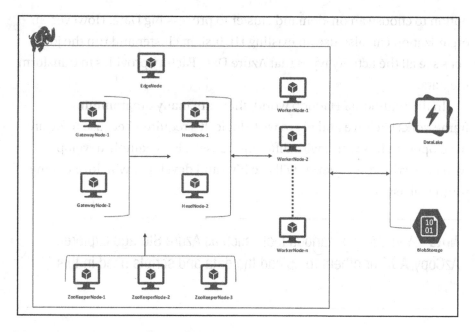

Figure 4-1. *HDInsight architecture*

HDInsight provides an enterprise-grade platform to process Big Data. These are some of its benefits:

- Easy to set up a cluster

- Scalability

- Enterprise-grade security

- Connection to various storage types on Azure

- Provider of various types of Hadoop clusters

- Monitor and logging

- Extensibility

Azure Data Factory makes life easier for an organization that wants to process Big Data on HDInsight but doesn't have enough expertise within the organization to set up a cluster. The platform provides an option to choose an on-demand cluster to process Big Data. However, an organization can also use an existing HDInsight cluster and run the job. Let's see all the activity types that Azure Data Factory provides to transform the data.

In the traditional Hadoop world, there are many programming frameworks like hive and pig to write logic. It's required because there are developers in this world with different skillsets. For example developer who love writing sql queries will use hive and developer who love writing script will use pig.

Note   You can use various tools such as Azure Storage Explorer, AzCopy, ADF, or others to upload the data and scripts used in this chapter.

Hive Activity

Apache Hive provides an abstraction layer to the developer to write SQL-like queries on the data.

Let's look at an example where you can leverage ADF to execute a Hive job. This example uses crime data (which is available by default when you set up an HDInsight cluster). Figure 4-2 shows the sample data.

	A	B	C	D	E	F	G	H	I	J	K	L	M	N	O
1	115856	Alaska	Anchorage	2007	284142	2405	22	257	453	1673	11107	1454	8397	1256	145
2	115857	Alaska	Bethel	2007	6488	61	2	15	0	44	107	25	63	19	2
3	115858	Alaska	Bristol Bay	2007	1028	8	0	0	0	8	49	11	24	14	1
4	115859	Alaska	Cordova	2007	2322	9	0	0	0	9	14	1	10	3	0
5	115860	Alaska	Craig	2007	1186	41	0	0	0	41	18	5	10	3	2
6	115861	Alaska	Dillingham	2007	2494	76	1	24	3	48	78	18	40	20	0
7	115862	Alaska	Fairbanks	2007	31287	258	5	43	42	168	1358	236	957	165	6
8	115863	Alaska	Haines	2007	2260	16	0	1	0	15	74	24	46	4	0
9	115864	Alaska	Homer	2007	5629	52	0	2	1	49	220	32	165	23	1
10	115865	Alaska	Houston	2007	1992	3	0	0	0	3	40	8	24	8	0
11	115866	Alaska	Juneau	2007	30746	126	1	22	17	86	1364	174	1137	53	10
12	115867	Alaska	Kenai	2007	7620	30	1	2	3	24	318	32	265	21	0
13	115868	Alaska	Ketchikan	2007	7384	21	0	9	1	11	476	41	407	28	4
14	115869	Alaska	Kodiak	2007	6242	33	0	5	1	27	209	13	175	21	6

Figure 4-2. *Sample crime data*

Figure 4-3 shows the Hive script.

```
CREATE EXTERNAL TABLE Crime(
        RowID int,
        State string,
        City string,
        Year int,
        Population int,
        ViolentCrime int,
        MurderAndNonEgligentManslaughter int,
        ForcibleRape int,
        Robbery int,
        AggravatedAssault int,
        PropertyCrime int,
        Burglary int,
        LarcenyTheft int,
        MotorVehicleTheft int,
        Arson int
) ROW FORMAT DELIMITED FIELDS TERMINATED BY ',' LOCATION 'wasb://rawdata@adfbookblobsampledata.blob.core.windows.net/';

INSERT OVERWRITE DIRECTORY  'wasb://hiveoutput@adfbookblobsampledata.blob.core.windows.net/out'
        SELECT State, Year, SUM(ViolentCrime) , SUM(Robbery), SUM(PropertyCrime) FROM Crime GROUP BY State, Year;
```

Figure 4-3. *Sample script*

Upload the sample data and Hive script to Azure Blob Storage.

In this example, you will be using an HDInsight on-demand cluster. Azure Data Factory needs permission to set up an HDInsight cluster on your behalf, so you need to provide the service principal to authenticate ADF.

Note   You need to be the owner or have Microsoft.Authorization/*/ Write access to assign an AD app.

---

1) Go to https://portal.azure.com.

2) Once logged in, click Azure Active Directory, then "App registrations," and then "New application registration" (see Figure 4-4).

Figure 4-4. *Azure AD app registration*

3) Enter an app name, select an application type, enter the sign-on URL, and click Create (see Figure 4-5).

Figure 4-5. *Azure AD app creation*

4) Once the Azure AD app is created, copy the application ID and click Settings (see Figure 4-6).

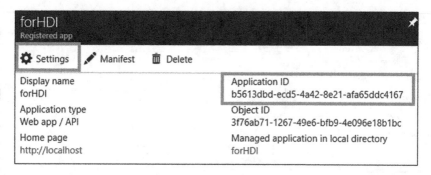

Figure 4-6. *Registered Azure AD app overview*

5) Create a new key; once it's saved, copy the value (see Figure 4-7).

Figure 4-7. *Azure AD app keys*

6) Close and go back to Azure Active Directory.

7) Click Properties and copy the directory ID (see Figure 4-8).

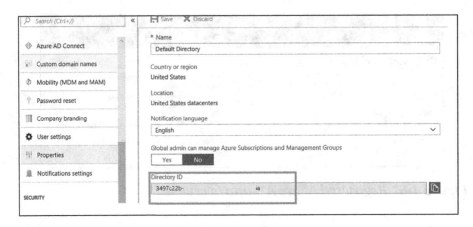

Figure 4-8. *Azure AD app properties*

At this stage, you have three values (see Table 4-1).

Table 4-1. *Azure AD App Values*

Name	Value
Service principal ID (application ID)	b5613dbd-ecd5-4a42-8e21-afa65ddc4167
Service principal key (key)	onNXXXXXXXXXXX42GOMF3F2OgzXXXXX1cizX/ObU7PQ=
Tenant (directory ID)	XXXXXXX-7189-XXXX-af2a-XXXXXXXXXX

8) Select Subscriptions and click the subscription (see Figure 4-9).

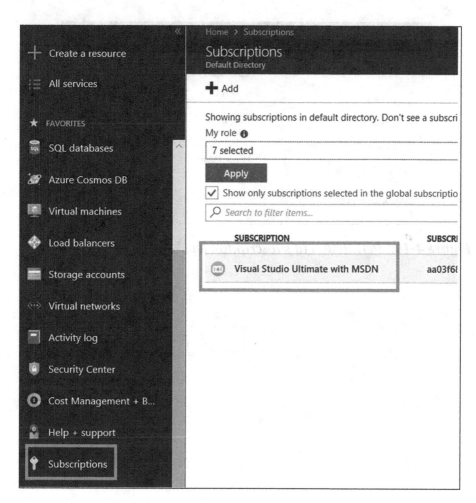

Figure 4-9. *Azure subscription information*

9) Select "Access control (IAM)" and click Add (see
    Figure 4-10).

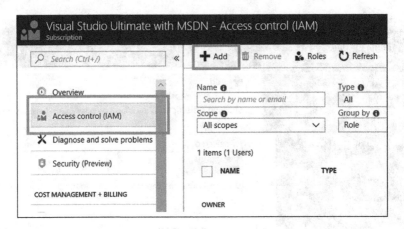

Figure 4-10. *Permission at subscription level*

10) Set Role to Contributor and select the application
created earlier (see Figure 4-11).

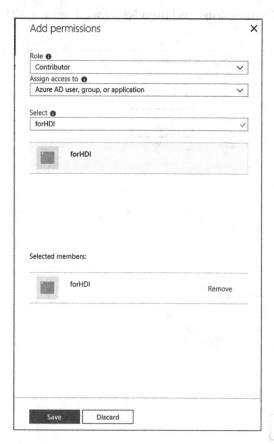

Figure 4-11. Adding permission

11)   Go to Azure Data Factory Services and click Author
      and Deploy.

12)   Click Connections and then New (see Figure 4-12).

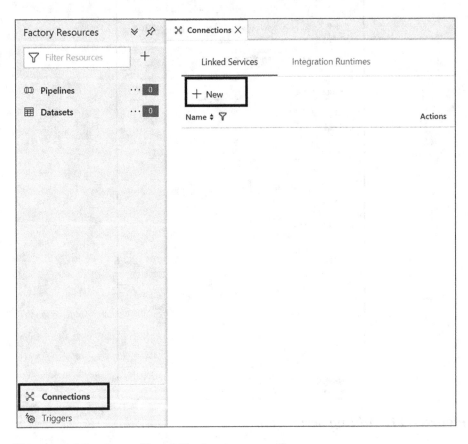

Figure 4-12. *Azure Data Factory connection*

13) Click Azure Blob Storage and then Continue (see Figure 4-13).

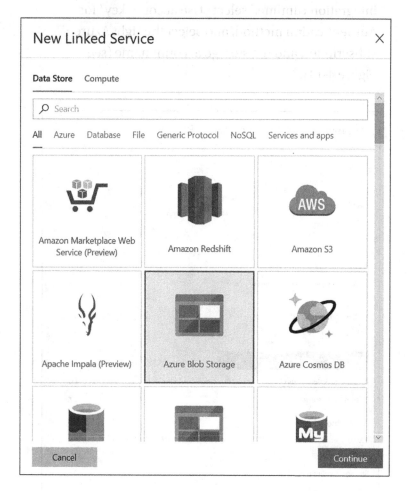

Figure 4-13. *Azure Data Factory linked service options*

14) Enter the name, select
AutoResolveIntegrationRuntime for "Connect via
integration runtime," select "Use account key" for
Authentication method, and select the right Azure
subscription and the storage account name (see
Figure 4-14).

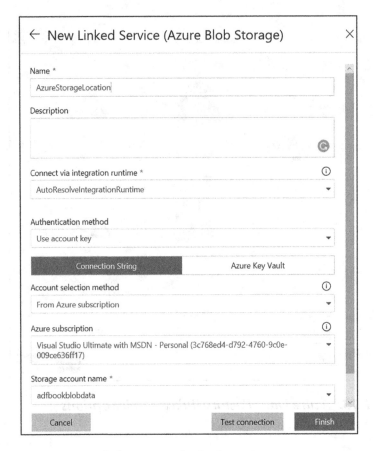

Figure 4-14. *Azure Blob Storage linked service*

15) Click Finish.

16) Click + and then Pipeline (see Figure 4-15).

Figure 4-15. *ADF pipeline*

17) Expand HDInsight and drag the Hive activity to the designer (see Figure 4-16).

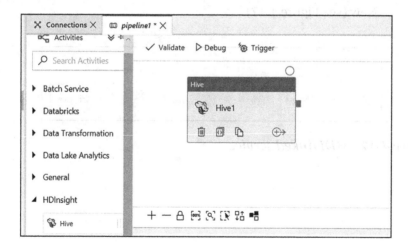

Figure 4-16. *Hive activity*

18)   On the General tab, provide the values in Table 4-2.

Table 4-2. *Hive Activity Values*

Property Name	Description
Name	Enter the activity name.
Description	Enter the activity description.
Timeout	Enter how long the activity runs. The default is seven days.
Retry	Enter how many times the activity keeps trying to run in case of any transient failure.
Retry Interval	Enter the difference between two retries.
Secure Output	Select if any output data shouldn't be logged.

19)   On the HDI Cluster tab, you need to configure ADF
to create an HDI cluster on the user's behalf. Click +
New (see Figure 4-17).

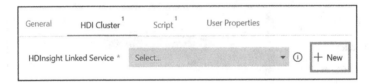

Figure 4-17. *HDI linked service*

Table 4-3 shows the properties to enter in the next window.

Table 4-3. *HDI Creation Values*

Property Name	Description
Description	Provide a description of the linked service.
Type	Select On-demand HDInsight.
Connect via integration runtime	Select AutoResolveIntegrationRuntime.
Azure Storage Linked Service	Storage use by the cluster to store and process data.
Cluster type	Select Hadoop as you are using Hive, which is part of the Hadoop cluster type
Cluster Size	1. Add more if the subscription has enough cores in the specified region.
Time to live	00:05:00 defines how long HDInsight lives after the completion of active jobs on the cluster. The default is five minutes.
Service principal Id	Provide the service principal ID created in the previous step.
Services principal key	Provide the service principal key created in the previous step.
Tenant	Prepopulated. This should match with the Azure AD ID.
Version	3.6 (the latest one).
Select region	Make sure enough cores are available to create a cluster.
Additional storage linked service	The general recommendation is to store the metadata and data in different storage.

20) Click Finish, and on the Script tab select the right
     script linked service, which is the storage link where
     scripts are stored. If you're not sure of the file path,
     then click Browse Storage to select the script (see
     Figure 4-18).

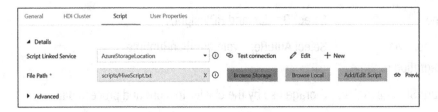

Figure 4-18. *Setting the Hive script path*

21) Let's skip Advance option however if require we can
     capture logs, pass argument, parameter and define
     variable under Advanced option.

22) Click Validate to make sure there are no errors (see
     Figure 4-19).

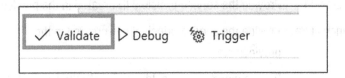

Figure 4-19. *Validating the ADF pipeline option*

23) Click Publish All (see Figure 4-20).

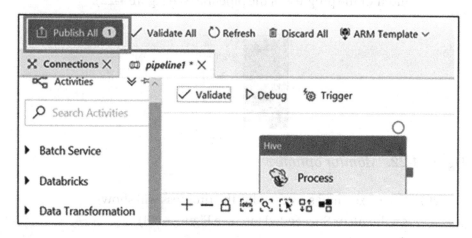

Figure 4-20. *Publishing changes*

24) Click Trigger Now and then Finish (see Figure 4-21).

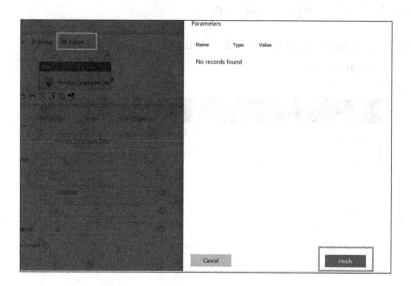

Figure 4-21. *Triggering the ADF pipeline*

25)   On the left, click the gauge icon (aka the Monitor) to monitor the progress of the pipeline (see Figure 4-22).

Figure 4-22.   *Monitor option*

26)   Once executed successfully, the progress will show on the All or Succeeded tab (see Figure 4-23).

Figure 4-23.   *ADF pipeline progress*

27)   The output will be stored in Azure Blob Storage (see Figure 4-24).

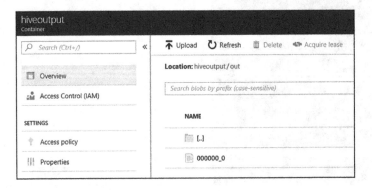

Figure 4-24.   *Output*

Pig Activity

There are developers who love to write scripts to process data, but it's easier to use the Pig activity. Let's consider the same data and use the Pig script to process data. See Figure 4-25.

```
crimedata = LOAD 'wasb://rawdata@adfbookblobsampledata.blob.core.windows.net/CrimeData.csv' USING PigStorage(',')
        AS (ROWID,State,City,Year,Population, ViolentCrime,MurderAndNonEgligentManslaughter, ForcibleRape,Robbery,AggravatedAssault,
        PropertyCrime, Burglary,LarcenyTheft,MotorVehicleTheft,Arson);

CrimeinAlaska = FILTER crimedata BY State == 'Alaska';

STORE CrimeinAlaska into 'wasb://pigoutput@adfbookblobsampledata.blob.core.windows.net/out' USING PigStorage (',');
```

Figure 4-25. *Pig script*

Let's set up the Azure Data Factory pipeline.

1) Switch to the ADF Author & Monitor UI. Remove the Hive activity and add a Pig activity (see Figure 4-26).

117

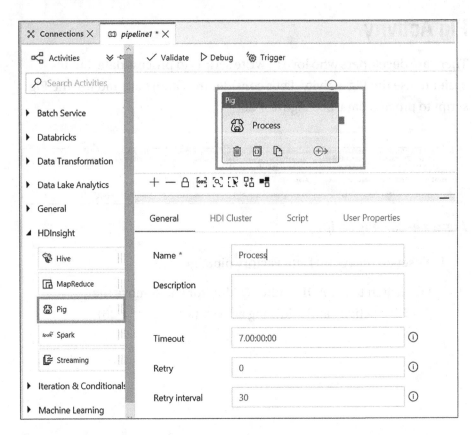

Figure 4-26. *Pig activity*

2) On the General tab, provide the values listed in
    Table 4-4.

Table 4-4. *Pig Activity Values*

Property Name	Value
Name	Enter the activity name.
Description	Enter the activity description.
Timeout	Enter how long the activity runs. The default is seven days.
Retry	Enter how many times the activity should keep trying to run in case of any transient failure.
Retry Interval	Enter the difference between two retries.
Secure Output	Select this if any of the output data shouldn't be logged.

3) On the HDI Cluster tab, set HDInsight Linked
    Service to HDILinkedServices (created earlier in this
    chapter), as shown in Figure 4-27.

Figure 4-27. *Setting the HDI linked service*

4)   Select the script (as shown in Figure 4-28).

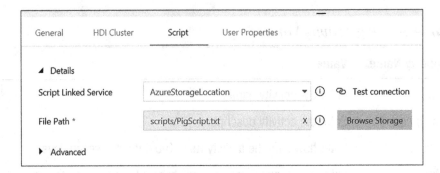

Figure 4-28. *Pig script path*

5)   Click Publish All (see Figure 4-29).

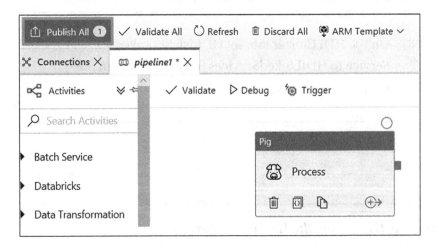

Figure 4-29. *Publishing the changes*

6)   Click Trigger Now (see Figure 4-30).

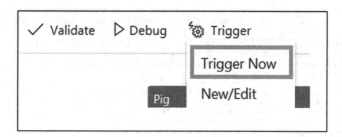

Figure 4-30. *Triggering the ADF pipeline*

7)   Click Finish.

8)   Click Monitor to watch the progress of the pipeline.

9)   Once the job has completed successfully,
the output will be available in Azure Blob Storage
(see Figure 4-31).

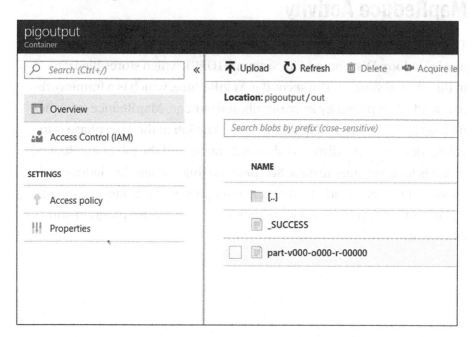

Figure 4-31. *Output location*

The output will look like Figure 4-32.

```
←   →   ↻        🔒  https://adfbookblobsampledata.blob.core.windows.net/pigoutput/out/part-

115856,Alaska,Anchorage,2007,284142,2405,22,257,453,1673,11107,1454,8397,1256,145
115857,Alaska,Bethel,2007,6488,61,2,15,0,44,107,25,63,19,2
115858,Alaska,Bristol Bay Borough,2007,1028,8,0,0,0,8,49,11,24,14,1
115859,Alaska,Cordova,2007,2322,9,0,0,0,9,14,1,10,3,0
115860,Alaska,Craig,2007,1186,41,0,0,0,41,18,5,10,3,2
115861,Alaska,Dillingham,2007,2494,76,1,24,3,48,78,18,40,20,0
115862,Alaska,Fairbanks,2007,31287,258,5,43,42,168,1358,236,957,165,6
115863,Alaska,Haines,2007,2260,16,0,1,0,15,74,24,46,4,0
115864,Alaska,Homer,2007,5629,52,0,2,1,49,220,32,165,23,1
115865,Alaska,Houston,2007,1992,3,0,0,0,3,40,8,24,8,0
115866,Alaska,Juneau,2007,30746,126,1,22,17,86,1364,174,1137,53,10
115867,Alaska,Kenai,2007,7620,30,1,2,3,24,318,32,265,21,0
115868,Alaska,Ketchikan,2007,7384,21,0,9,1,11,476,41,407,28,4
115869,Alaska,Kodiak,2007,6242,33,0,5,1,27,209,13,175,21,6
115870,Alaska,North Pole,2007,1869,9,0,1,1,7,116,24,85,7,0
115871,Alaska,North Slope Borough,2007,6569,70,0,15,7,48,149,52,70,27,8
115872,Alaska,Palmer,2007,7931,65,0,4,1,60,282,23,242,17,2
115873,Alaska,Petersburg,2007,2890,1,0,0,0,1,117,6,103,8,0
115874,Alaska,Seward,2007,3054,3,0,1,0,2,146,21,118,7,2
115875,Alaska,Sitka,2007,8932,31,0,9,0,22,290,21,250,19,2
115876,Alaska,Skagway,2007,827,1,0,0,0,1,14,1,11,2,0
```

Figure 4-32. *Output*

MapReduce Activity

The Apache Hadoop framework is distributed via two services. The first one is Hadoop Distributed File System (HDFS), which stores Big Data in distributed storage. The second is MapReduce, which is a framework that reads data parallelly from distributed storage. MapReduce is further divided into two parts: Map and Reduce. The job of the Map phase is to collect data from the distributed storage node, and the job of the Reduce phase is to aggregate the data. So, there are times when the Hadoop developer needs to perform different data processing. Hadoop provides a platform for developers to write their own map reduce program and execute it.

Azure Data Factory provides the MapReduce activity to run your own map reduce program. Let's run a Big Data "Hello World" program (also known as WordCount).

1) Copy `hadoop-mapreduce-examples.jar` and `davinci.txt` into the same Azure Blob Storage (created earlier in this chapter), as shown in Figure 4-33.

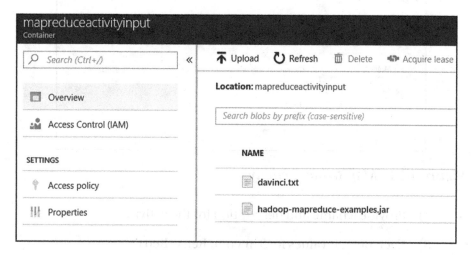

Figure 4-33. *Storage to store data and JAR file*

2) Switch to the ADF Author & Monitor UI and remove any activity present there.

3) Add the MapReduce activity (see Figure 4-34).

Figure 4-34. *MapReduce activity*

4) Provide a name and description for the activity.

5) Keep default values for Timeout, Retry, Retry
    Interval, and Secure Output.

6) On the HDI Cluster tab, set HDInsight Linked
    Service to HDILinkedServices (created earlier in this
    chapter).

7) On the Jar tab, for the JAR linked service, link to the storage where the JAR file was copied. Set the class name to wordcount, and for the file path, click Browse Storage and select the JAR file. For the arguments, provide the input file and output location (make sure the output container does not exist). Here is how the argument looks (see Figure 4-35):

```
wasb://mapreduceactivityinput@adfbookblobsampledata.
blob.core.windows.net/davinci.txt wasb://
mapreduceactivityoutput@adfbookblobsampledata.blob.
core.windows.net/
```

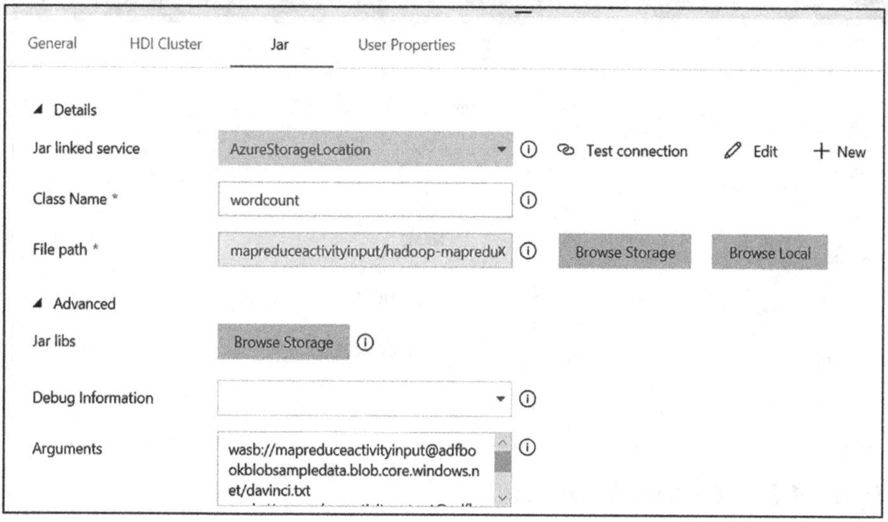

Figure 4-35. Setting up a location

8) Leave Parameter and User Properties as they are.

9) Click Publish All.

10) Click Trigger and then Trigger Now.

11) Click Finish.

12) Switch to the Monitor to check the progress of pipeline execution (see Figure 4-36).

Figure 4-36. *ADF pipeline monitor*

13) Once the pipeline executes successfully, the output will be presented in Azure Blob Storage (see Figure 4-37).

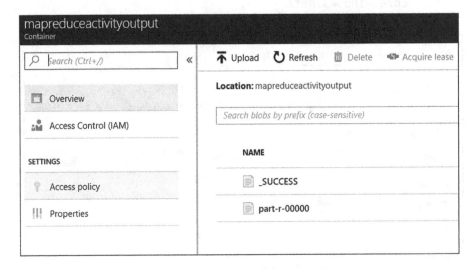

Figure 4-37. *Output location*

14) Open the file named part-r-00000 (see Figure 4-38).

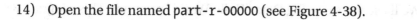

```
←  →  ↻        🔒 https://adfbookblobsampledata.blo

"(Lo)cra"       1
"1490   1
"1498,"  1
"35"     1
"40,"    1
"AS-IS".        1
"A_      1
"Absoluti       1
"Alack! 1
"Alack!"        1
"Alla   1
"Allegorical    1
"Alpine-glow"   1
"And    2
"Antoni 1
"At     1
"B_     1
"Bathers        1
"Bononiae       1
"By     1
"Come   1
"De     1
"Defects".      1
"Description    1
"Disposizione   2
"Doctrinal      1
"E      1
"Egli   1
"El     1
"Elements".     1
"Every  1
"Facetie        2
"First  1
"Formulario     1
"Here   1
"How    1
"I      11
```

Figure 4-38. *Output*

Streaming Activity

Apache Hadoop was written on Java platform. All map reduce jobs should be written in the Java programming language. However, Hadoop provides a streaming API for MapReduce that enables developers to write map and reduce functions in languages other than Java.

We'll use the same Big Data "Hello World" program. This program will count the total number of words in an input file.

1) Copy the following files into a container: `davinci. txt`, `mapper.exe`, and `reduce.exe` (see Figure 4-39).

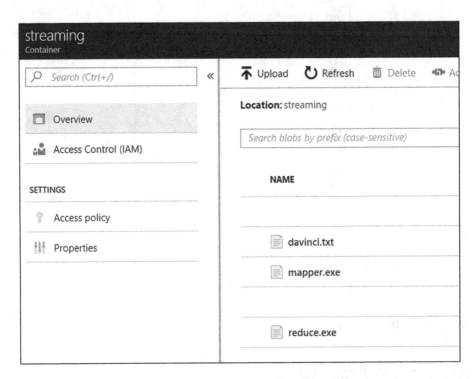

Figure 4-39. *Container to store data and executable*

2) Switch to the ADF Author & Monitor UI and remove any activity present there.

3)   Add the Streaming activity (see Figure 4-40).

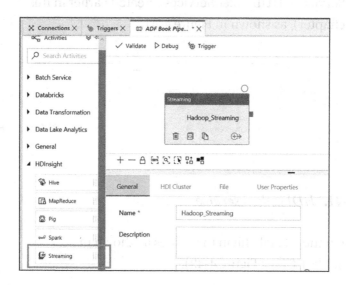

Figure 4-40.   *Streaming activity*

4)   On the General tab, provide the values in Table 4-5.

Table 4-5.   *Streaming Activity Values*

Property Name	Value
Name	Enter the activity name.
Description	Enter the activity description.
Timeout	Enter how long the activity runs. The default is seven days.
Retry	Enter how many times the activity should keep trying to run in the case of any transient failure.
Retry Interval	Enter the difference between two retries.
Secure Output	Select this if any output data shouldn't be logged.

5) On the HDI Cluster tab, set HDInsight Linked
Service to HDILinkedServices (created earlier in this
chapter), as shown in Figure 4-41.

Figure 4-41. *HDI linked service*

6) On the File tab, fill in the values as shown in
Table 4-6 (see Figure 4-42).

Table 4-6. *Streaming Activity Values*

Property	Value
Mapper	Use mapper.exe.
Reducer	Use Reduce.exe.
File Linked Service	Specify AzureStorageLocation.
File path for Mapper	Click Browse Storage and point to streaming/mapper.exe.
File path for Reducer	Click Browse Storage and point to streaming/reducer.exe.
Input	Enter wasbs://streaming@adfbookblobsampledata.blob.core. windows.net/davinci.txt.
Output	The output is wasbs://streaming@adfbookblobsampledata. blob.core.windows.net/output/wc.txt.

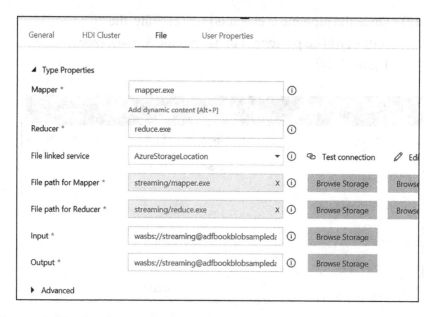

Figure 4-42. *Setting up a streaming activity*

7) Leave Parameter and User Properties as they are.

8) Click Publish All.

9) Click Trigger and then Trigger Now.

10) Click Finish.

11) Switch to the Monitor to check the progress of the pipeline execution (see Figure 4-43).

Figure 4-43. *Monitoring the ADF pipeline*

12) Once the pipeline is executed successfully, the output will be presented in Azure Blob Storage (see Figure 4-44).

Figure 4-44. *Output location*

13) Open the file named part-00000 to view the total number of words in an input document.

Spark Activity

Apache Spark provides primitives for in-memory cluster computing. The main difference between Spark and Hadoop is that Spark uses memory and can use the disk for data processing, whereas Hadoop uses the disk for processing.

Azure Data Factory provides a Spark activity (that can run on an HDInsight cluster) for data transformation. In this example, assume you received data from all the stores and you want to figure out what the average sale is for each store. In this example, let's explore how to leverage an existing HDInsight cluster to build this small solution.

1) Switch to Azure.

2) Click "Create a resource."

3) Click Analytics (see Figure 4-45).

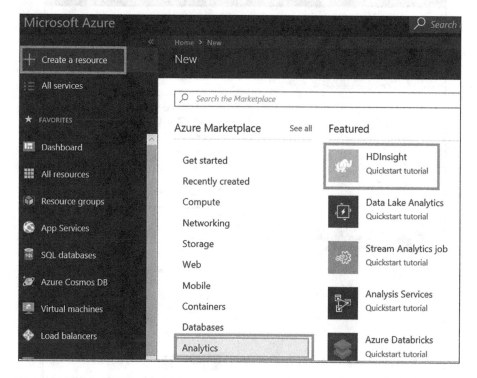

Figure 4-45. *HDI service*

4) Click HDInsight.

5) Provide a cluster name.

6) Select your subscription.

7) Select the cluster type (Spark 2.x on Linux [HDI]).

8) Provide the cluster login information.

9) Select or create the resource group.

10) Select the location (choose the location where you already created ADF services), as shown in Figure 4-46.

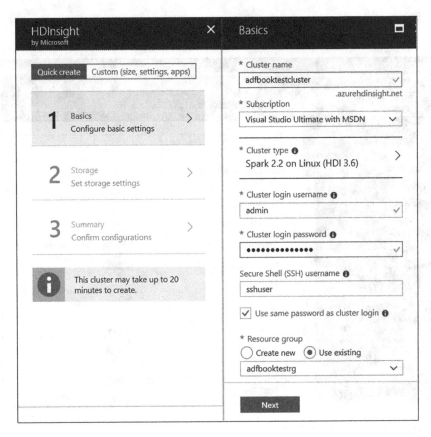

Figure 4-46. *HDI cluster creation*

Note   If you don't want to go with a default size of HDInsight, then switch to the "Custom (size, settings, apps)" option.

---

11) Create a new storage account.

12) On the summary page, click Create.

13) Once the HDInsight cluster is created, open Azure
Blob Storage, which is connected to HDInsight.

14) Create a new container (see Figure 4-47).

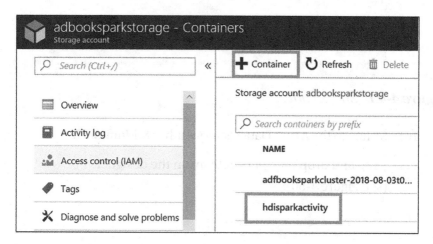

Figure 4-47. *Container creation*

15) Under the newly created container, copy the
PySpark file and the sample data (see Figure 4-48).

	All_Sales_Records.csv
☐	main.py

Figure 4-48. *Data and code*

`All_Sales_Records.csv` contains sample data, and `main.py` contains Spark code (see Figure 4-49).

```
from pyspark.sql import SparkSession

spark = SparkSession.builder \
    .appName("HDISpark-ADF")\
    .enableHiveSupport()\
    .getOrCreate()

from pyspark.sql import *

from pyspark.sql.types import *

from pyspark.sql.functions import *

salesData = spark.read.csv('wasb://hdisparkactivity@adbooksparkstorage.blob.core.windows.net/All_Sales_Records.csv', header=True,

resultData = salesData.select(col('StoreId') , col('TotalDue') ).groupBy('StoreId').avg('TotalDue')

resultData.repartition(1).write.csv('wasb://hdisparkactivity@adbooksparkstorage.blob.core.windows.net/SalesAvg' , header=True)
```

Figure 4-49. *Spark code*

16) Switch to the Azure Data Factory Author & Monitor UI.

17) Drag and drop the Spark activity on the designer (see Figure 4-50).

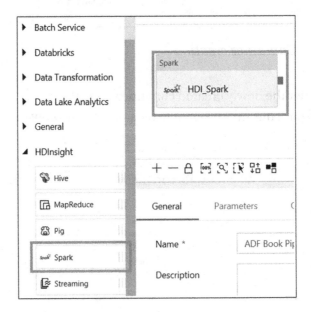

Figure 4-50. *Spark activity*

18) Click the General tab.

19) Provide the name and add a description.

20) Use the defaults for the rest of the properties (see Figure 4-51).

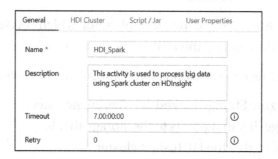

Figure 4-51. *Setting up an HDI Spark activity*

21) Click HDI Cluster.

22) Click +New (see Figure 4-52).

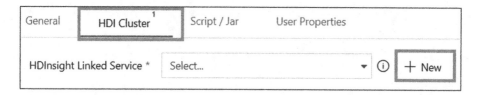

Figure 4-52. *Setting up an cluster for HDI Spark activity*

23) Provide a named for the cluster and add a description.

24) Select Bring your own HDInsight for Type.

25) Don't change default values for "Connect via integration runtime."

26) Select "From Azure subscription" for "Account selection method."

27) Select the Azure subscription where you created the HDInsight cluster.

28) Select the HDI cluster.

29) Provide the user name (administrator, which you set up while creating the HDInsight cluster).

30) Select the Password option and provide the password.

31) For Azure Storage Linked Service, create a new storage link that points to the storage that is connected to the HDInsight cluster.

32) Click "Test connection" to make sure all settings are valid.

33) Click Finish (see Figure 4-53).

Figure 4-53. *Provide HDI cluster details*

You can either use a script or add a fat JAR for data processing. In this example, we'll focus on providing a script for data processing.

1) Click Script/Jar.

2) Select Script for Type.

3) Select the storage where you stored the script for Job Linked Service.

4) Select the path and main.py file for File Path (see Figure 4-54).

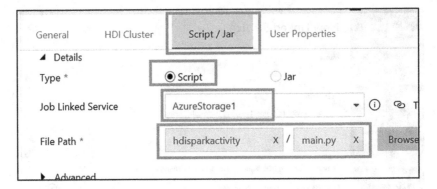

Figure 4-54. *Setting up script for HDI Spark activity*

5)   Click Publish All (see Figure 4-55).

Figure 4-55. *Publishing the changes*

6)   Click Trigger and then Trigger Now.

7)   Click Finish.

8)   Switch to the Monitor tab on the left side to monitor the job (see Figure 4-56).

Triggered By Type	Triggered By	Status	Parameters
Manual	Manual trigger	⟳ In Progress...	

Figure 4-56. *Monitoring the ADF pipeline progress*

9)   Once you succeed, investigate Azure Blob Storage, and you will find the files in Figure 4-57.

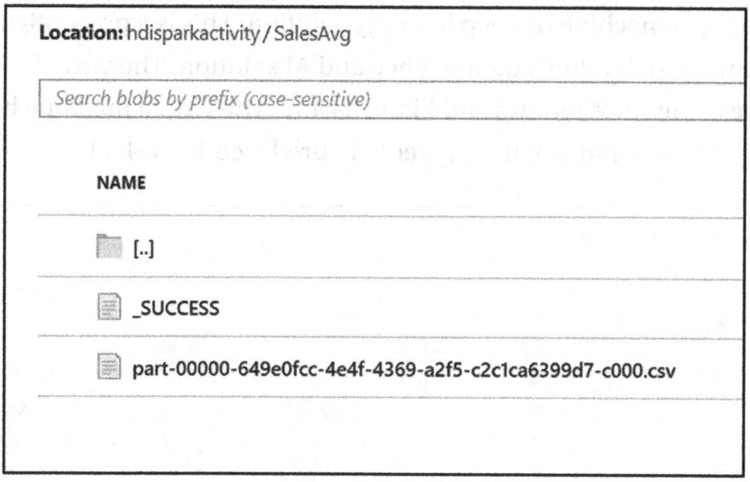

Location: hdisparkactivity / SalesAvg

Search blobs by prefix (case-sensitive)

NAME

[..]

_SUCCESS

part-00000-649e0fcc-4e4f-4369-a2f5-c2c1ca6399d7-c000.csv

Figure 4-57. *Output*

10)   Click the last file (the one that starts with part-00000.) and download it to view the results.

Azure Machine Learning

Data capture helps business analytics provide insight on the present and the past. With machine business analytics, you can get insight into the future. This means the industry is moving from basic analytics to advanced capabilities. Businesses need to be proactive to take the necessary steps to avoid any issues, which is leading to transformational changes. Some examples of machine business analytics are product recommendations, predictive maintenance, demand forecasting, market basket analysis, and so on. There are various case studies available in various domains that show how companies can take advantage of Big Data.

As shown in Figure 4-58, you can use various services such as Spark, SQL Server (on-premises), and Azure Machine Learning to build a model. Microsoft also provides a data science virtual machine in cases where you are building a machine or deep learning solution. This is a preconfigured environment to develop a data science and AI solution. The virtual machine comes in Windows and Linux flavors. The virtual machine has some of the tools and languages preconfigured (see Table 4-7).

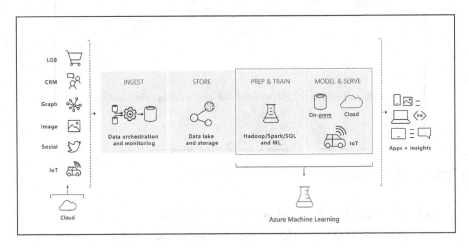

Figure 4-58. *AI development lifecycle .*

Table 4-7. *Tools and Language Support in Data Science VM*

Tools				Language
Microsoft R Open	Apache Drill	Git and Gitbash	PyTorch	R
Microsoft ML Server	Xgboost	OpenJDK	Keras	Python
Anaconda Python	RStudio Desktop	TensorFlow	Theano	Julia
JuliaPro	RStudio Server	Juno	Chainer	C#
Jupyter Notebook	Weka	H2O	MXNet	Java
Visual Studio code	Rattle	Light GBM	Horovod	JS
PyCharm	Atom	Vims and Emacs	CNTK	

Microsoft Azure Machine Learning makes the entire process easy. As a newbie, instead of wasting a lot of time reading, setting up the environment, and working in development and with deployment models, you can quickly get started with Azure Machine Learning. Its user interface makes it super easy to build and deploy AI solutions. You can preprocess your data, choose from various algorithms, deploy, and make it available as a web service. There are various built-in solutions available in the Microsoft AI gallery (`https://gallery.azure.ai`). However, if you are a professional, you can still utilize the R language, the Python language, and the OpenV library within Azure Machine Learning Studio.

Let's understand the use case and build a solution.

AdventureWorks wants to leverage the data to understand which products the customers tend to purchase together. This will help them place products together on a shelf. For example, if you purchase bread from a store, then chances are high you'll also buy milk/butter/jam/egg from there. However, if these items are kept far apart or on another floor, then chances are very low you will buy them, which can impact sales.

You'll use Microsoft Azure Machine Learning to build this solution and leverage Azure Data Factory to orchestrate the pipeline.

The architecture of the solution will look like Figure 4-59.

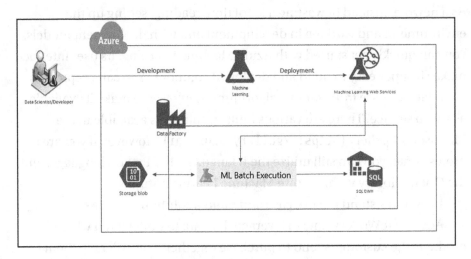

Figure 4-59. *Reference architecture*

Let's start with Microsoft Azure Machine Learning.

1) Go to `https://gallery.azure.ai`.

2) Search for *Discover Association Rules*
    (see Figure 4-60).

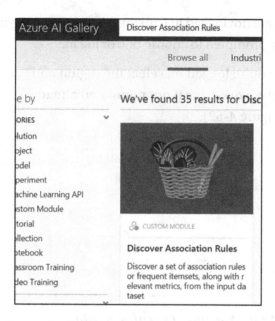

Figure 4-60. *Azure AI Gallery*

3) Click Discover Association Rules.

4) Click Open in Studio (see Figure 4-61).

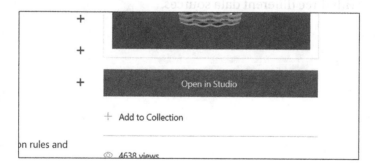

Figure 4-61. *Opening in Studio*

145

5) If you are not logged in with an existing account, you will be prompted to choose one or log in.

6) Once you're logged in, select the region and then the workspace if not populated already (see Figure 4-62).

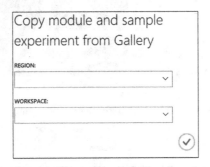

Figure 4-62. *Azure Machine Learning Studio*

7) Click OK.

8) Machine Learning Studio will look like Figure 4-63. It shows how to use the Discover Association Rule with three different data sources.

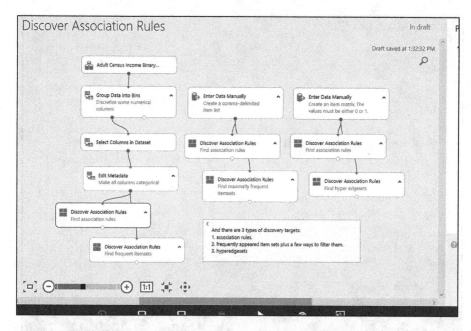

Figure 4-63. *Azure Machine Learning Studio with Discover Association Rule*

9) Delete all experimental items except one: the
    Discover Association Rules item (see Figure 4-64).

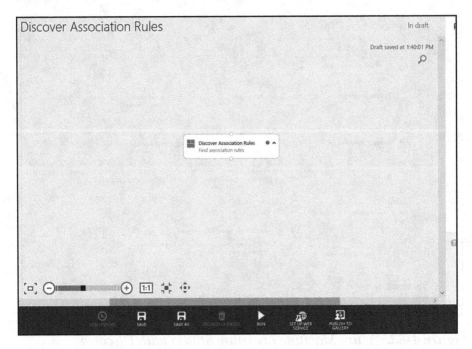

Figure 4-64. *Keeping the Discover Association Rules item*

10) Upload data to pass as an input to the Discover
     Association Rules item.

11) Click +New (see Figure 4-65).

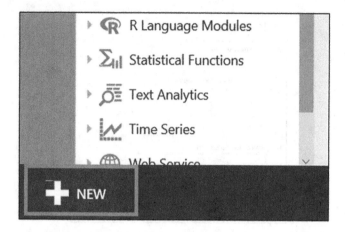

Figure 4-65. *Clicking +New*

12) Click Dataset and then From Local File (see Figure 4-66).

Figure 4-66. *Clicking From Local File*

13) Select a file to upload (see Figure 4-67).

Figure 4-67. Selecting a file to upload

14)   Click OK.

15)   From Experiments, click Saved Datasets and then
      My Datasets (see Figure 4-68).

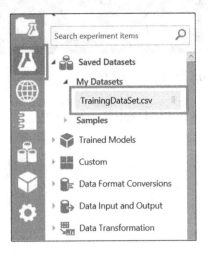

Figure 4-68. My Datasets list

16) Drag and drop `TrainingDataSet.csv` and link it
     with Discover Association Rules (see Figure 4-69).

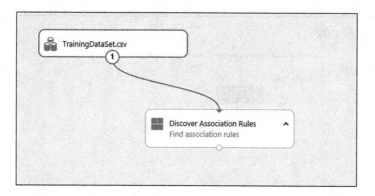

Figure 4-69. *Linking the two*

17) Select Discover Association Rules, and on the
     right side click "Launch column selector"
     (see Figure 4-70).

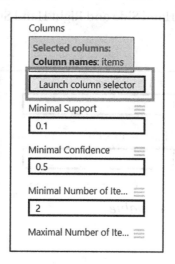

Figure 4-70. *Launching a column selector*

18) Select the column named Pname and click OK (see Figure 4-71).

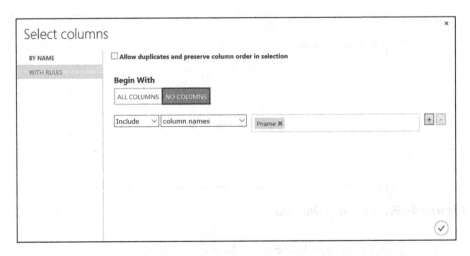

Figure 4-71. *Selecting a column*

19) Scroll down and make sure there are no values given for Left Hand Side and Right Hand Side (see Figure 4-72).

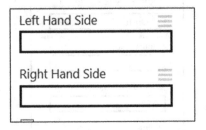

Figure 4-72. *Clearing the values*

20)   Click Run (see Figure 4-73).

Figure 4-73. *Clicking Run*

21)   Once completed, the experiment will look like Figure 4-74.

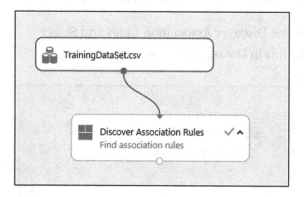

Figure 4-74. *The progress so far*

22)   On the left side, drag and drop Select Columns in Dataset (see Figure 4-75).

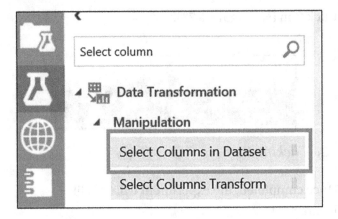

Figure 4-75. *Selecting Select Columns in Dataset*

23) Link the Discover Association Rules and Select Columns in Dataset items (see Figure 4-76).

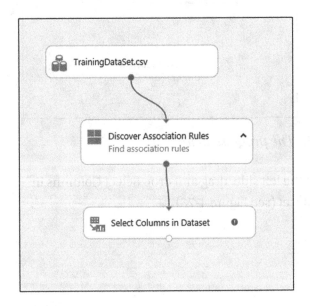

Figure 4-76. *Linking the two*

24) Click Select Columns in Dataset.

25) Click "Launch column selector" (see Figure 4-77).

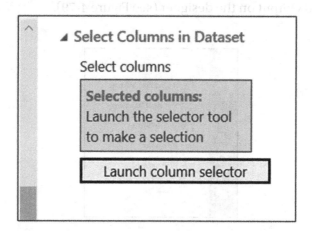

Figure 4-77. *Launching the column selector*

26) Select lhs and rhs from the list (see Figure 4-78).

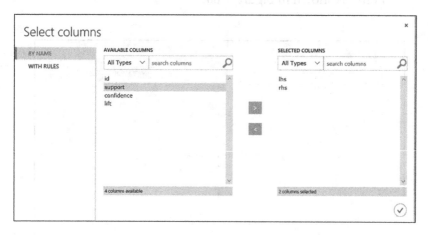

Figure 4-78. *Selecting lhs and rhs*

27) Click OK.

28) Let's add the web service input and output. This will allow the service to take input, process it, and present the results.

29) In the left pane, look for Web Service and drop Input and Output on the designer (see Figure 4-79).

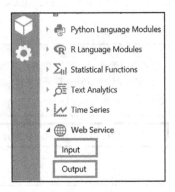

Figure 4-79. *Adding Input and Output*

30) Link the Input and Output items with the existing items as shown in Figure 4-80.

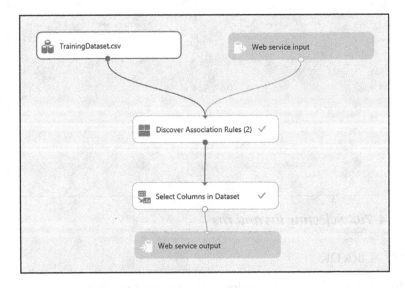

Figure 4-80. *Linking the items*

31) Click Run.

32) Click Deploy Web Service (see Figure 4-81).

Figure 4-81. *Clicking Deploy Web Service*

33) Once completed, click New Web Service Experience
to get a web service endpoint and access key (see
Figure 4-82).

discover association rules

DASHBOARD   CONFIGURATION

General   New Web Services Experience preview

Published experiment

View snapshot   View latest

Description

No description provided for this web service.

API key

Default Endpoint

API HELP PAGE	TEST
REQUEST/RESPONSE	Test Test preview
BATCH EXECUTION	Test preview

Figure 4-82. *Clicking New Web Service Experience*

34)   Click "Use endpoint" (see Figure 4-83).

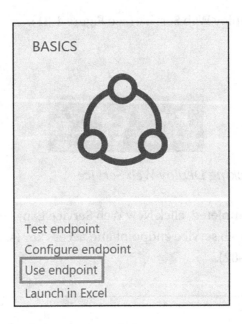

Figure 4-83. *Endpoint management*

35)   Copy the primary key and batch requests value and
store them somewhere. You'll use this information
when creating the ADF pipeline (see Figure 4-84).

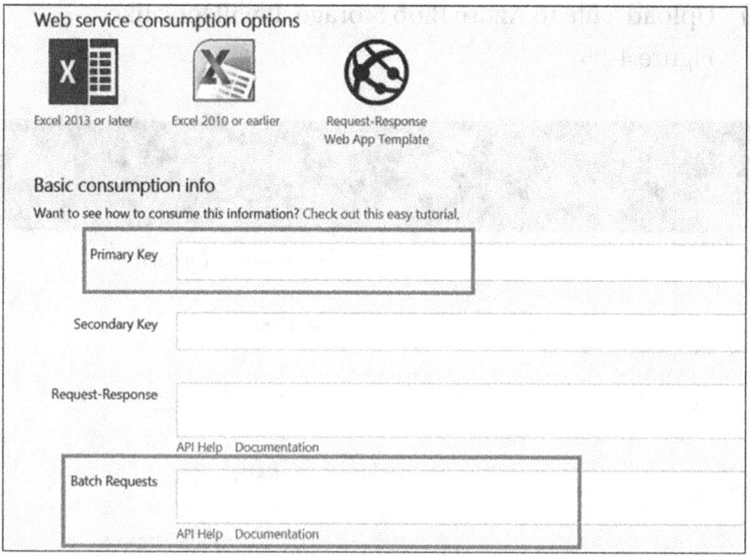

Figure 4-84. *Primary key and batch requests*

Now you'll upload retail customers' bill information on Azure
Blob Storage.

1) Upload a file to Azure Blob Storage. It will look like Figure 4-85.

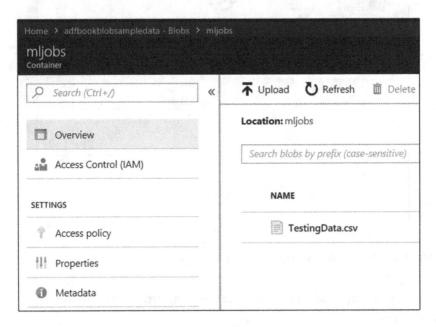

Figure 4-85. *Container to store test data*

Let's create a table in SQL Datawarehouse to capture the output of Azure ML.

1) Run the query shown in Figure 4-86.

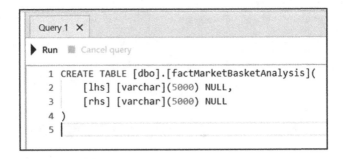

Figure 4-86. *Creating a table script*

Let's create an Azure Data Factory pipeline.

1) Switch to the Azure Data Factory Author &
   Monitor UI.

2) Under Machine Learning, drag and drop ML Batch
   Execution on designer, as shown in Figure 4-87.

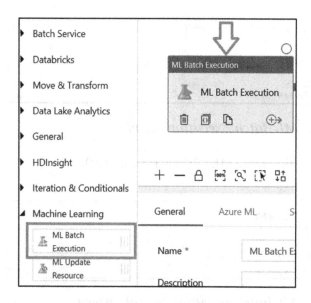

Figure 4-87.   *Azure Data Factory ML Batch Execution activity*

3) On the General tab, provide a name and add a
   description. Leave the default values for the rest of
   the properties (see Figure 4-88).

General	Azure ML	Settings	User Properties
Name *	ML Batch Execution		
Description			
Timeout	7.00:00:00		ⓘ
Retry	0		ⓘ
Retry interval	30		ⓘ

Figure 4-88. *ML Batch Execution activity*

4)   Click the Azure ML tab (see Figure 4-89).

Figure 4-89. *ML batch execution linked service*

5)   Provide the Azure ML linked service's name and description.

6)   Provide the endpoint that was copied earlier.

7)   Provide the API key that was copied earlier.

8)   Click Disable Update Resource as you are not updating the Azure Machine Learning model.

9)   Click "Test connection" (see Figure 4-90).

Figure 4-90. *Testing the connection*

10)   Under Settings, fill in the settings under Web Service
       Inputs and Web Service Outputs, as shown in
       Figure 4-91.

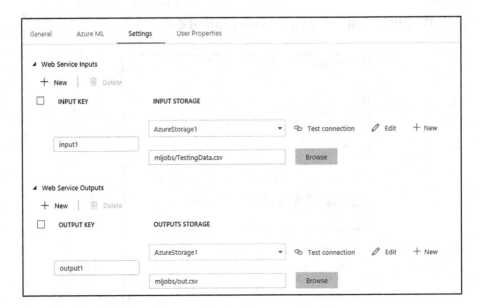

Figure 4-91. *ML batch execution activity setting*

11) Drag and drop the Copy Data activity and connect it
with the ML Batch Execution activity (on success),
as shown in Figure 4-92.

Figure 4-92. *Connecting activities*

12) Select the Copy Data activity, click the Source gab (this will connect to the file location, which is the output location of the ML Batch Execution activity (see Figure 4-93).

Figure 4-93. *Setting the Copy activity*

13) Create the Azure SQL Data Warehouse connection, as shown in Figure 4-94.

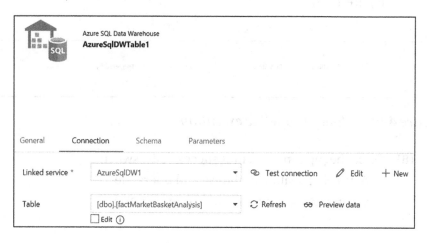

Figure 4-94. *Azure SQL Data Warehouse connection*

14) Click Mapping and then Import Schemas (see
Figure 4-95).

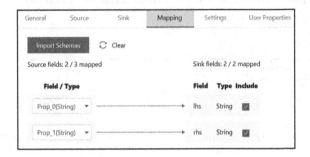

Figure 4-95. *Field mapping*

15) Click Publish All.

16) Click Trigger and then Trigger Now.

17) Switch to the Monitor to watch the progress (see
Figure 4-96).

Figure 4-96. *Monitor pipeline execution*

18) Once the pipeline executes successfully, switch
to Azure SQL Data Warehouse and query the
factMarketBasketAnalysis table (Figure 4-97).

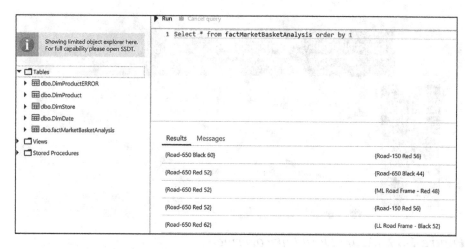

Figure 4-97. Querying the database

Azure Data Lake

Azure Data Lake is an on-demand analytics job service. This service has two layers underneath: Azure Data Lake storage and Azure Data Lake Analytics. As the name suggests, the first one is used to store unlimited data, and the other is used as compute on Big Data. Both the services provide various features such as security at a granular level, unlimited storage and compute, pay per job, an easy framework to develop jobs, and various language and monitoring capabilities. People often called it *Big Data as a service*.

Why does this matter to any organization when there is another Big Data framework already available? Many organizations don't have the resources to build Big Data solutions, they don't do Big Data analytics too often, or they want to focus more on solution building than understanding technology.

It's not necessary to use both services at the same time. If organizations want, they can use an Azure Data Lake store as storage and deploy HDInsight on top of it for computation. See Figure 4-98.

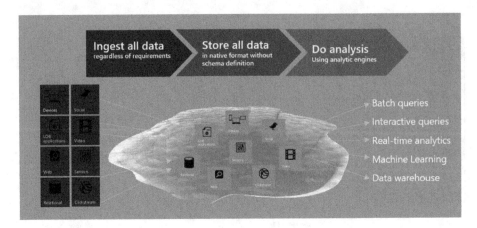

Figure 4-98. *Azure Data Lake overview*

Azure Data Factory provides a Data Lake Analytics activity for data transformation. Let's first set up Azure Data Lake storage (see Figure 4-99).

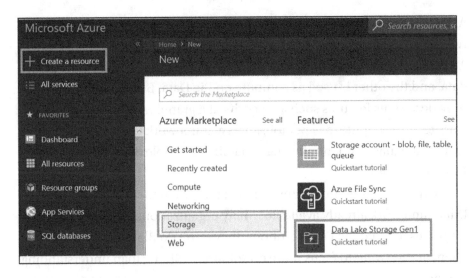

Figure 4-99. *Selecting the storage*

1) Switch to the Azure portal.

2) Click "Create a resource."

3) Click Storage.

4) Click Data Lake Storage Gen1.

5) Provide a name for the service.

6) Select your subscription.

7) Create or select a resource group.

8) Select the location.

9) Select the pricing package.

10) Select the encryption settings.

11) Click Create (see Figure 4-100).

Figure 4-100. Setting up the storage

12) Once it's created, click and open the service in the portal.

13) Click "Data explorer."

14) Click the storage you just created (see Figure 4-101).

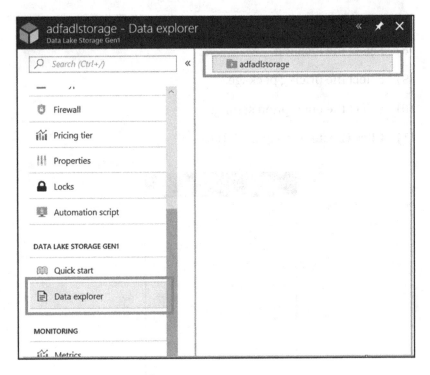

Figure 4-101. *Data explorer*

15)   Click Upload (see Figure 4-102).

Figure 4-102. *Azure Data Lake storage options*

16)   Upload the All_Sales_Records.csv file (see
       Figure 4-103).

NAME	SIZE
All_Sales_Records.csv	87.7 MB

Figure 4-103. *Sample data*

Now let's set up the Azure Data Lake Analytics account.

1)   Switch to the Azure portal.

2)   Click "Create a resource."

3)   Click Analytics.

4)   Click Data Lake Analytics (see Figure 4-104).

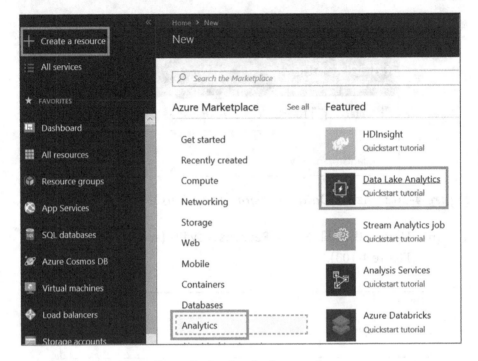

Figure 4-104. *Azure Data Lake Analytics service*

5) Provide the name of the account.

6) Select your subscription.

7) Create or select a resource group.

8) Select the location (the same as you selected for storage).

9) Select the storage name created in the earlier step for Data Lake Storage Gen1 (you can also skip the earlier step and create the storage directly from here).

10) Select the pricing package.

11) Click Create (see Figure 4-105).

Figure 4-105. *Options for Azure Data Lake Analytics*

The Azure Data Lake Analytics linked service requires a service principal authentication to connect to the Azure Data Lake Analytics service. Let's set up the Azure AD app registration and grant permission to access an Azure Data Lake account. At the end of this setup, you will get the service principal ID, key, and tenant ID.

1) Switch to the Azure portal.

2) Click Azure Active Directory,

3) Click "App registrations."

4) Click "New application registration" (see Figure 4-106).

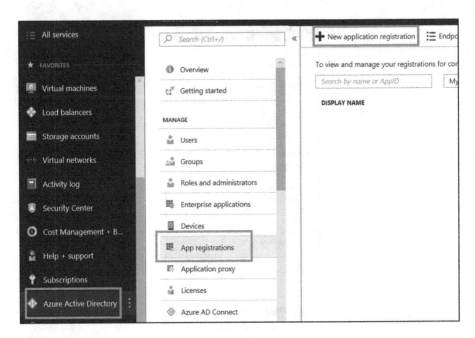

Figure 4-106. *Azure AD app registration*

5) Provide the name.

6) Set "Application type" to "Web app / API."

7) Provide the sign-on URL.

8)   Click Create (see Figure 4-107).

Figure 4-107. *Creating the app*

9)   Click the newly created app (see Figure 4-108).

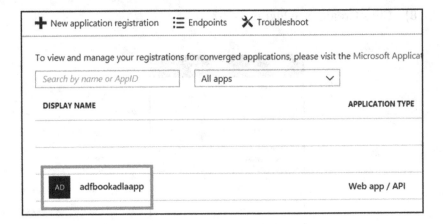

Figure 4-108.   *Opening the app settings*

10)   Copy the application ID.

11)   Click Settings.

12)   Click "Required permissions."

13)   Click +Add (see Figure 4-109).

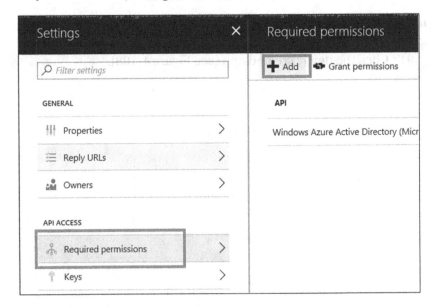

Figure 4-109.   *Setting permissions*

14) Click Select an API.

15) Select the Azure Data Lake API.

16) Click Select (see Figure 4-110).

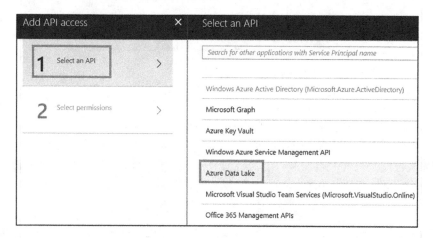

Figure 4-110. *API selection*

17) Select the correct permissions on step 2.

18)   Click Select (see Figure 4-111).

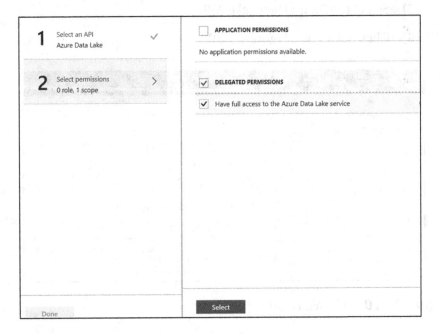

Figure 4-111. *Permission settings*

19)   Click Done.

20)   Select Keys.

21)   Provide a description.

22)   Provide an expiration date; this is the expiry date attributed to the key.

23)   Click Save.

24)   Once it's saved, the service will show a key value. Copy the value to Notepad as it will not show up once it's closed (see Figure 4-112).

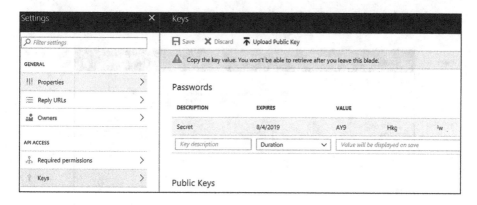

Figure 4-112. *Setting up the keys*

25) Open the Azure Data Lake Analytics service.

26) Click "Add user wizard" (see Figure 4-113).

Figure 4-113. *Granting permission to the user*

27) Click "Select user."

28) Select the Azure AD app created earlier.

29)   Select the app and click Select (see Figure 4-114).

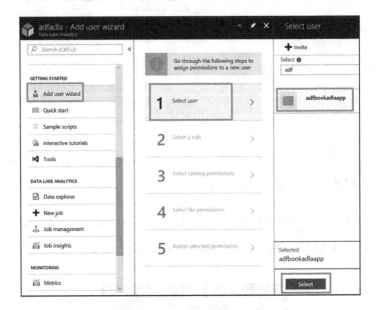

Figure 4-114. *User selection*

30)   Select Data Lake Analytics Developer for "Select a role" (see Figure 4-115).

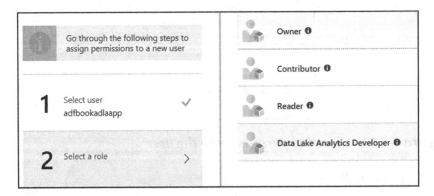

Figure 4-115. *Role options*

31) For step 3, don't change the default value, and click Select.

32) For step 4, provide permission to "This folder and all children" (see Figure 4-116).

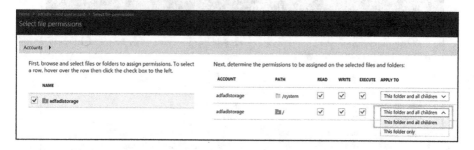

Figure 4-116. *Permission settings*

33) On step 5, click Run (see Figure 4-117).

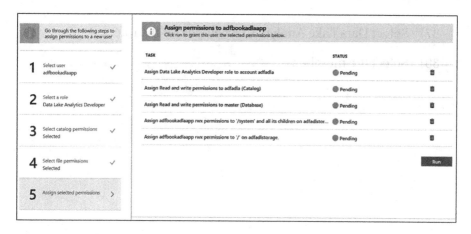

Figure 4-117. *Permission assignment*

34) Click Done.

35) Click "Access control (IAM)."

36) Click +Add (see Figure 4-118).

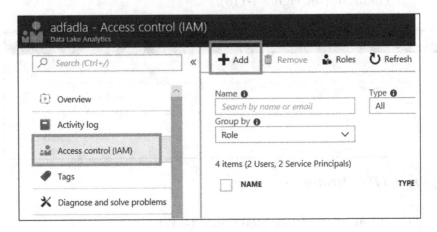

Figure 4-118. *Adding user access*

37) Select Data Lake Analytics Developer for the role.

38) Select the member.

39)   Click Save (see Figure 4-119).

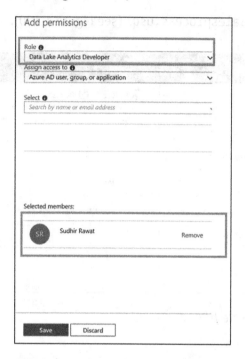

Figure 4-119. *Member selection*

Let's upload a script to Azure Blob Storage.

1) Upload `salesprocess.usql` (see Figure 4-120).

Figure 4-120. *Code file*

Figure 4-121 and Figure 4-122 show the U-SQL code.

```
 1  DECLARE @inputfile   string = "/All_Sales_Records.csv";
 2  DECLARE @outputfile1 string = "/StorewiseSales.csv";
 3  DECLARE @outputfile2 string = "/popularProducts.csv";
 4
 5  @schemadef =
 6      EXTRACT SalesOrderID     int,
 7          StoreId int,
 8          OrderDate    DateTime,
 9          SubTotal     decimal,
10          Taxperc      int,
11          TaxAmt          decimal,
12          Freightperc              int,
13          Freight      decimal,
14          TotalDue     decimal,
15          SalesOrderDetailID   int,
16          PName    string,
17          OrderQty     int,
18          UnitPrice    decimal,
19          UnitPriceDiscount    decimal,
20          LineTotal decimal
21      FROM @inputfile
22      USING Extractors.Csv(skipFirstNRows:1);
```

Figure 4-121. *U-SQL code*

```
23
24 @res1 =
25     SELECT
26         StoreId,
27         SUM(TotalDue) AS TotalDue
28     FROM @schemadef
29     GROUP BY StoreId;
30
31 @res2 =
32     SELECT
33         PName, COUNT(*) AS maximum_time
34     FROM @schemadef
35     GROUP BY PName;
36
37 OUTPUT @res1 TO @outputfile1
38 USING Outputters.Csv(outputHeader:true);
39
40 OUTPUT @res2 TO @outputfile2
41 USING Outputters.Csv(outputHeader:true);
```

Figure 4-122. *U-SQL code, continued*

Let's set up Azure Data Factory to run and schedule the pipeline.

1) Switch to the Azure Data Factory Author & Monitor UI.

2) Drag and drop a U-SQL activity onto the designer
   (see Figure 4-123).

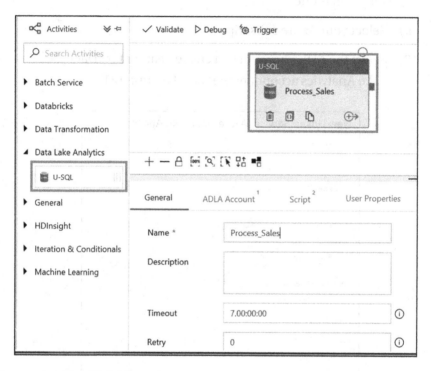

Figure 4-123. *U-SQL activity*

3) Click the General tab and provide a name and
   description of the activity.

4) Click the ADLA Account tab.

5) Click New.

6)   Provide the name and add a description.

7)   Select AutoResolveIntegrationRuntime for "Connect via integration runtime."

8)   Select Subscription for the Data Lake Analytics selection mode.

9)   Select your Azure subscription.

10) Select the ADLA account you created earlier for "Data Lake Analytics account name" (see Figure 4-124).

Figure 4-124. *Setting up the U-SQL activity*

11) Provide a tenant (directory ID). Ideally, it is populated by default.

12) Provide a service principal ID (the application ID from the Azure AD app registered earlier) and service principal key (the key from the Azure AD app registered earlier).

13) Click "Test connection."

14) If the connection is successful, click Finish (see
     Figure 4-125).

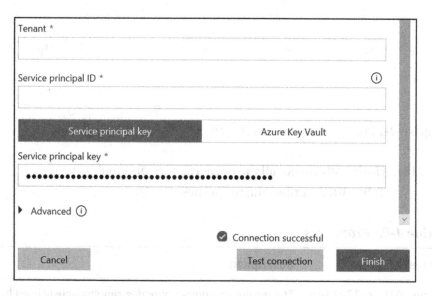

Figure 4-125. *Configuring the U-SQL activity*

15) Click the Script tab.

16) Select the Script linked service, which is the location
     of storage where you uploaded the script file. If
     the link is not available, create a "New storage link
     service."

17) Click Browse Storage to choose the U-SQL script
     path (see Figure 4-126).

Figure 4-126. *Setting the script path*

18)   Under Advanced, all the properties are optional.
Table 4-8 describes the properties.

Table 4-8. *Properties*

Property	Description
degreeOfParallelism	The maximum number of nodes simultaneously used to run the job.
Priority	The lower the number, the higher the priority.
Parameters	Parameters to pass into the U-SQL script.
runtimeVersion	Runtime version of the U-SQL engine to use.
compilationMode	Semantic: Only perform semantic checks and necessary sanity checks. Full: Perform the full compilation, including syntax check, optimization, code generation, etc. SingleBox: Perform the full compilation, with the TargetType setting to SingleBox. If you don't specify a value for this property, the server determines the optimal compilation mode.

19) Click Publish All.

20) Click Trigger and then Trigger Now.

21) Once the ADF pipeline has run successfully, switch to Azure Data Lake Storage to find out the result (a CSV file), as shown in Figure 4-127.

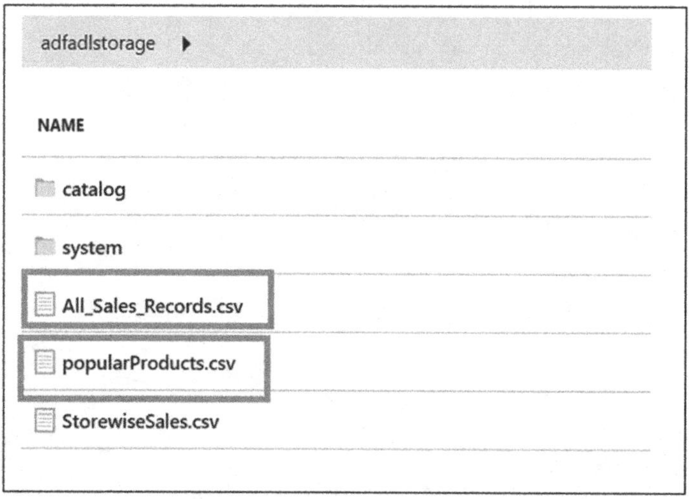

Figure 4-127. *Output*

This chapter focused on how to build data transformation solutions using various activities in Azure Data Factory. The chapter focused on HDInsight, Azure Machine Learning, and Data Lake activities. All services were provided by Microsoft Azure. What if you want to run data transformation code in Python? Let's move to the next chapter and find out.

CHAPTER 5

Data Transformation: Part 2

In the previous chapter, you worked with various activities to build a solution with various data analytics requirements. On Microsoft Azure, you will notice that many services are available for storage and compute. There is no right or wrong choice of service; you just need to be clear about what the business needs now and, more important, what it needs in the future. There will always be trade-offs when choosing one service over another. So, as a data professional, you need to be clear on what the business requirements are now and in the future.

Most data professionals want to know whether they can schedule their open source code for data transformation? That is the question this chapter will answer through building a pipeline to process data using Python.

Before diving into generating more code, let's take a look at two different terms that are frequently used.

Data Warehouse to Modern Data Warehouse

In the traditional sense, a *data warehouse* is a central repository that consolidates data from different sources such as a file system, a customer relationship management (CRM) system, SQL Server, and so on. The data is cleaned and transformed, the values are calculated, and the data is stored for historical purposes. This has been going on for a decade.

© Sudhir Rawat and Abhishek Narain 2019
S. Rawat and A. Narain, *Understanding Azure Data Factory*,
https://doi.org/10.1007/978-1-4842-4122-6_5

Today, there are many more data points generating data, and it's becoming useful to utilize this data. In addition to getting data from on-premises sources, you also can get data from social media platforms and third-party APIs. Therefore, you need a scalable and high-compute system that can retrieve data from these sources and store it in a data warehouse. Figure 5-1 shows a modern data warehouse pattern.

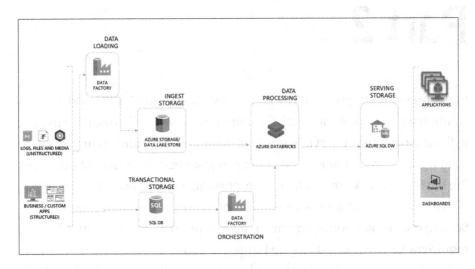

Figure 5-1. *Modern data warehouse pattern*

ETL vs. ELT

Extract-transform-load (ETL) and extract-load-transform (ELT) are not new to data professionals. Both techniques describe transformations, either before loading or after loading the data. In ELT, the transformation happens on the target, whereas in ETL, it may happen on the source side or on a compute layer in between. If you are processing Big Data, you may want to use ETL and then use an Azure Databricks Spark cluster to transform the data in an optimized environment with lower latency. If you have the same source and destination, you can leverage the compute power of a system like Azure SQL Data Warehouse to transform data there. Since ELT takes place in the first stage of loading raw data on the target, you can leverage of the power of a system like Azure SQL Data Warehouse to transform the data parallelly.

As there is no right or wrong way to process data, you may want to look at various parameters such as the data source and destination, latency, scalability, performance, cost, skill set, and so on, to decide on ETL or ELT. This chapter will show how to apply both approaches using Azure Data Factory.

Azure Databricks

Apache Spark is one of the most contributed to projects in the Apache world. Apache Spark uses an in-memory engine to process Big Data and makes it upto 100 times faster than Hadoop. The best part of the technology is that it has a runtime engine, and on top of the engine there are various libraries available such as SparkSQL, GraphX, Streaming, and the machine learning libraries. Bringing this platform on-premises, configuring it, and building a security and collaboration layer is a tedious task. That's where Azure Databricks comes into the picture and provides an optimized platform to run Spark jobs. The beauty of Azure Databricks is that it helps set up the environment in less time, streamlines workflows, and provides a collaboration workspace between the data scientist, data engineer, and data analyst. Figure 5-2 shows the architecture of Azure Databricks.

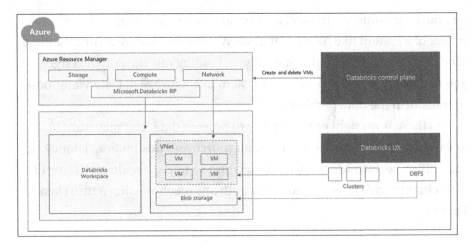

Figure 5-2. *Azure Databricks architecture on Azure*

Here are the benefits of using Azure Databricks:

- Optimized environment

- Ease of setup and management

- Provides enterprise security through Azure AD integration

- Collaboration

- PowerBI integration

- Integrates with other Azure services

When should you choose HDInsight Spark versus Azure Databricks? Both are optimized to run Spark workloads. HDInsight provides a platform-as-a-service (PaaS) experience where organizations can run multiple types of workloads such as Kafka, Spark, MapReduce, Storm, HBase, and Hive LLAP. Azure Databricks supports only Spark clusters. The platform provides a software-as-a-service (SaaS) experience. Also, it helps different people within the organization to collaborate easily. The pricing of the services is another consideration.

Build and Implement Use Case

In this use case, you will focus on transforming data using Azure Data Factory. This will be an example of ETL.

AdventureWorks wants to operationalize its data pipeline so that the company can visualize data seamlessly without worrying about the platform. Through this chapter and the previous chapter, each step is broken down separately so that it is easy to understand the solution. If required, you can put together all the blocks and build one ADF pipeline. The following are the services used in this demo:

- Microsoft Azure Data Factory

- Microsoft Azure SQL Data Warehouse (DWH)

- Microsoft Azure Databricks

- Microsoft Azure Blob Storage

One of the ways to load dimension data is to use Azure Data Factory's Copy activity to transfer dimension data to Azure SQL Data Warehouse. The other way is to leverage Azure Databricks to do it (as shown in Figure 5-3). You can do various kinds of transformations such as managing slowly changing dimensions (SCD-1, SCD-2, SCD-3) and checking for data anomalies.

For the AdventureWorks retail company, you'll build the solution shown in Figure 5-3 to move all the dimension data. In this scenario, you are ingesting data from a CSV file.

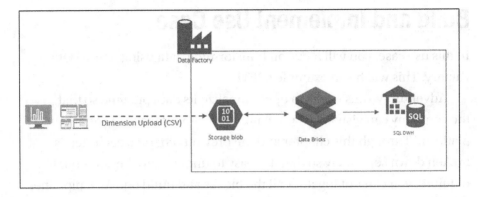

Figure 5-3. *Architecture to feed dimension data*

Let's upload the CSV files to Azure Blob Storage. You can use Azure Data Factory (the Copy Data activity) as we discussed in previous Chapter to move data to Azure Blob Storage. Figure 5-4 shows the files.

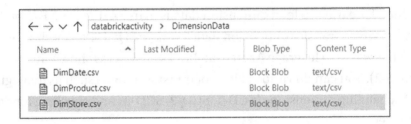

Figure 5-4. *Dimension/master data files*

Let's set up Azure SQL Data Warehouse.

1) Go to `https://portal.azure.com`.

2) Click "Create a resource."

3) Click Databases.

4) Click SQL Data Warehouse (see Figure 5-5).

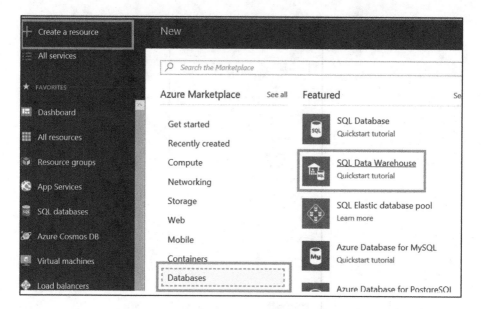

Figure 5-5. *Selecting SQL Data Warehouse*

5) Provide the database name.

6) Select your subscription.

7) Create or select a resource group.

8) Set "Select source" to "Blank database."

9) Create a new server.

10) Select your needed performance level.

11) Leave Collation at its default value.

12) Click Create (see Figure 5-6).

Figure 5-6. Providing values to set up the SQL Data Warehouse service

13) Once created, click SQL Data Warehouse.

14) Click "Query editor (preview)," as shown in
     Figure 5-7.

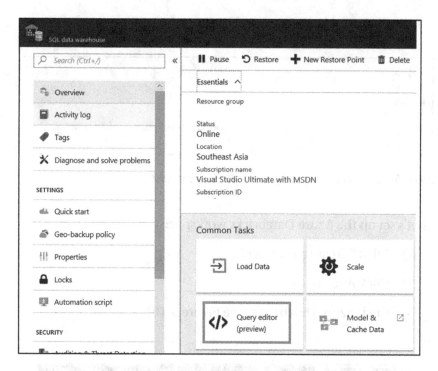

Figure 5-7. *Opening the query editor to run queries*

15)   Click Login (see Figure 5-8).

Figure 5-8. *Logging into SQL Data Warehouse*

16)   Enter the following command:

```
CREATE master KEY encryption BY password = 'adfBook@123';
go
```

17) Click Run (see Figure 5-9).

Figure 5-9. Executing scripts in the query editor

Let's set up the Azure Databricks workspace.

1) Click "Create a resource."

2) Click Analytics.

3) Click Azure Databricks (see Figure 5-10).

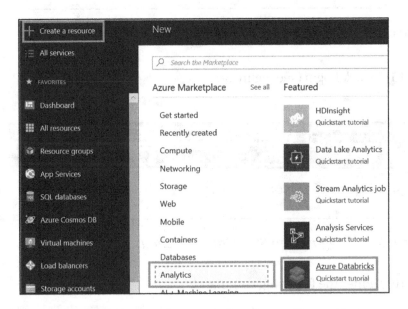

Figure 5-10. Selecting the Azure Databricks service

4) Provide the workspace name.

5) Select your subscription.

6) Create or select a resource group.

7) Select your location.

8) Select the needed pricing tier. For this demonstration, let's select Standard.

9) Click Create (see Figure 5-11).

Figure 5-11. *Providing values to set up Azure Databricks*

10) Click Azure Databricks Service in the Azure dashboard.

11) Click Launch Workspace (see Figure 5-12).

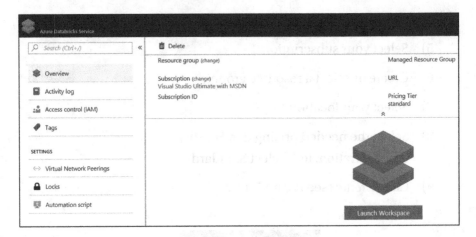

Figure 5-12. *Azure Databricks' Launch Workspace option*

12)   Click New Notebook (see Figure 5-13).

Figure 5-13. *Creating a new notebook*

13) Provide the name.

14) For Language, select Scala (see Figure 5-14).

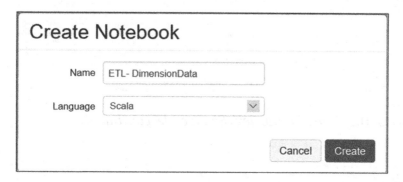

Figure 5-14. Creating a notebook

15) Click Create.

16) Once the notebook is created, paste the code
    shown in Figure 5-15, Figure 5-16, Figure 5-17, and
    Figure 5-18 into the notebook.

Figure 5-15. Azure Databricks Scala code

```
27  //Writing Error Records To Azure SQL DWH
28  dimproductErrorDF.write
29    .format("com.databricks.spark.sqldw")
30    .option("url",
      "jdbc:sqlserver://SQL_DWH_SERVER_NAME.database.windows.net:1433;database=SQL_DWH_DB_NAME;user=USER_NAME@SQL_DWH_SERVER_NAME;password=SQL_DWH_PASSWORD;encrypt=true;trustServer
      Certificate=false;hostNameInCertificate=*.database.windows.net;loginTimeout=30;")
31    .option("forward_spark_azure_storage_credentials", "true")
32    .option("dbTable", "DimProductERROR")
33    .option("tempDir", "wasbs:// CONTAINER_NAME@STORAGE_NAME.blob.core.windows.net/tempdata")
34    .save()
35
36  //Writing Valid Records To Azure SQL DWH
37  dimproductDF.write
38    .format("com.databricks.spark.sqldw")
39    .option("url",
      "jdbc:sqlserver://SQL_DWH_SERVER_NAME.database.windows.net:1433;database=SQL_DWH_DB_NAME;user=USER_NAME@SQL_DWH_SERVER_NAME;password=SQL_DWH_PASSWORD;encrypt=true;trustServer
      Certificate=false;hostNameInCertificate=*.database.windows.net;loginTimeout=30;")
40    .option("forward_spark_azure_storage_credentials", "true")
41    .option("dbTable", "DimProduct")
42    .option("tempDir", "wasbs://CONTAINER_NAME@STORAGE_NAME.blob.core.windows.net/tempdata")
43    .save()
44
45  // Loading DimStore
46  val DimStore_file_location = "wasbs:// CONTAINER_NAME@STORAGE_NAME.blob.core.windows.net/DimensionData/DimStore.csv"
47  val dimstoreDF = spark.read.format("csv").option("inferSchema", "true").option("header", "true").load(DimStore_file_location)
48
```

Figure 5-16. *Azure Databricks Scala code, continued*

```
49  dimstoreDF.write
50    .format("com.databricks.spark.sqldw")
51    .option("url",
      "jdbc:sqlserver://SQL_DWH_SERVER_NAME.database.windows.net:1433;database=SQL_DWH_DB_NAME;user=USER_NAME@SQL_DWH_SERVER_NAME;password=SQL_DWH_PASSWORD;encrypt=true;trustServerC
      ertificate=false;hostNameInCertificate=*.database.windows.net;loginTimeout=30;")
52    .option("forward_spark_azure_storage_credentials", "true")
53    .option("dbTable", "DimStore")
54    .option("tempDir", "wasbs:// CONTAINER_NAME@STORAGE_NAME.blob.core.windows.net/tempdata")
55    .save()
56
57  // Loading DimDate
58  //Instead of using inferSchema =true which eventually read records to find datatype of a column. Since we know the schema of this table hence we are defining and //applying
      schema
59
60  val schema = new StructType()
61    .add("id",IntegerType,true)
62    .add("DateId",IntegerType,true)
63    .add("Date",DateType,true)
64    .add("Year",IntegerType,true)
65    .add("Month",IntegerType,true)
66    .add("Day",IntegerType,true)
67    .add("MonthName",StringType,true)
68    .add("MonthNameShort",StringType,true)
69    .add("weekDay",StringType,true)
70    .add("WeekDayShort",StringType,true)
71    .add("DayOfWeek",IntegerType,true)
72    .add("Quarter",IntegerType,true)
73    .add("QuarterFormat",StringType,true)
74    .add("DayOfYear",StringType,true)
75    .add("WeekNumber",IntegerType,true)
76    .add("WeekNumberFormat",StringType,true)
77
```

Figure 5-17. *Azure Databricks Scala code, continued*

```
78
79  val DimDate_file_location = "wasbs:// CONTAINER_NAME@STORAGE_NAME.blob.core.windows.net/DimensionData/DimDate.csv"
80  val dimdateDF = spark.read.format("csv").schema(schema).option("header", "true").load(DimDate_file_location)
81
82  dimdateDF.write
83    .format("com.databricks.spark.sqldw")
84    .option("url",
      "jdbc:sqlserver://SQL_DWH_SERVER_NAME.database.windows.net:1433;database=SQL_DWH_DB_NAME;user=USER_NAME@SQL_DWH_SERVER_NAME;password=SQL_DWH_PASSWORD;encrypt=true;trustServerC
      ertificate=false;hostNameInCertificate=*.database.windows.net;loginTimeout=30;")
85    .option("forward_spark_azure_storage_credentials", "true")
86    .option("dbTable", "DimDate")
87    .option("tempDir", "wasbs:// CONTAINER_NAME@STORAGE_NAME.blob.core.windows.net/tempdata")
88    .save()
89
90  //End
91
```

Figure 5-18. *Azure Databricks Scala code, continued*

Let's set up Azure Data Factory.

1) Switch to the Azure Data Factory Author & Monitor UI.

2) Drag and drop a Notebook activity onto the designer (see Figure 5-19).

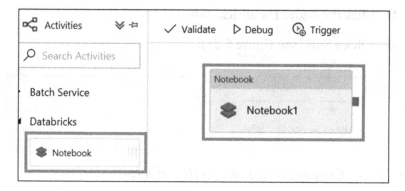

Figure 5-19. *Setting up an activity in Azure Data Factory*

3)   Name the activity (see Figure 5-20).

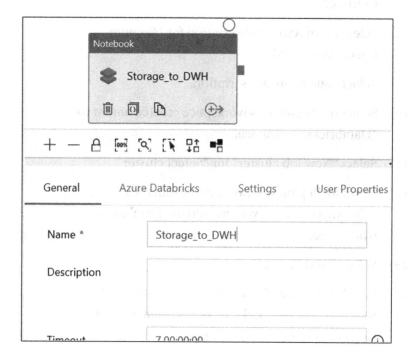

Figure 5-20. *Setting up an activity*

4)   Click the Azure Databricks tab.

5)   Click +New (see Figure 5-21).

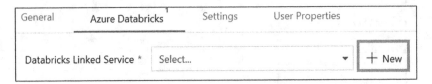

Figure 5-21. *Creating a Databricks linked service*

6)   Provide the name and add a description.

7)   Leave the default value for "Connect via integration runtime."

8)   Select From Azure Subscription for "Account selection method."

9)   Select your Azure subscription.

10)   Select the Databricks workspace created earlier for "Databricks workspace."

11)   Select "New job cluster" for "Select cluster."

12)   Domain/Region will populate automatically. The value was set when you created the Databricks workspace.

13)   Select the access token.

14)   For "Access token," click the text box; it will take you to the Azure Databricks account to generate a token. Copy the token and paste it here.

15)   Select the cluster node type.

16) Select 4.1 (which includes Apache Spark 2.3.0 and Scala 2.11) for "Cluster version."

17) Select 1 for Workers (see Figure 5-22).

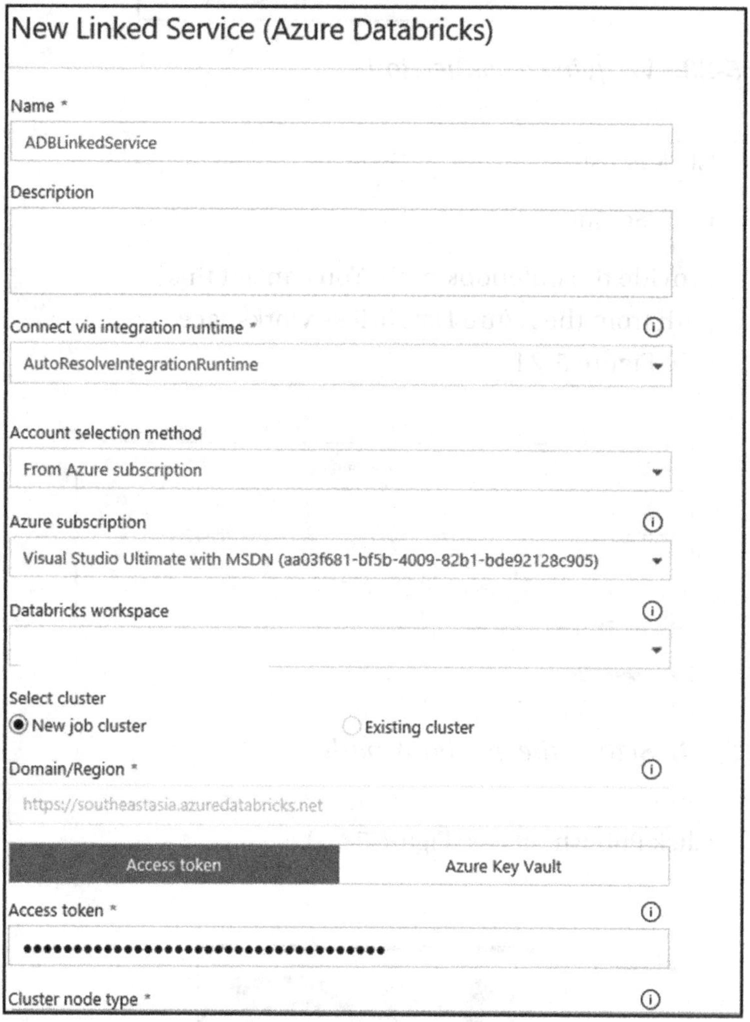

New Linked Service (Azure Databricks)

Name *

ADBLinkedService

Description

Connect via integration runtime *   ⓘ

AutoResolveIntegrationRuntime   ▼

Account selection method

From Azure subscription   ▼

Azure subscription   ⓘ

Visual Studio Ultimate with MSDN (aa03f681-bf5b-4009-82b1-bde92128c905)   ▼

Databricks workspace   ⓘ

▼

Select cluster
◉ New job cluster   ○ Existing cluster

Domain/Region *   ⓘ

https://southeastasia.azuredatabricks.net

Access token	Azure Key Vault

Access token *   ⓘ

●●●●●●●●●●●●●●●●●●●●●●●●●●●●●●●●●●●●●●●

Cluster node type *   ⓘ

Figure 5-22. Setting up a linked service

18)   Click "Test connection" (see Figure 5-23).

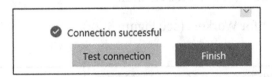

Figure 5-23. *Verifying a connection*

19)   Click Finish.

20)   Click Settings.

21)   Provide the notebook path. You can get this
path from the Azure Databricks workspace
(see Figure 5-24).

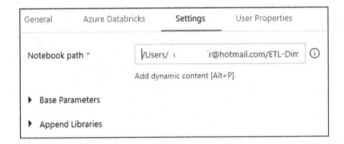

Figure 5-24. *Setting the notebook path*

22)   Click Publish All (see Figure 5-25).

Figure 5-25. *Setting up the activity*

23) Click Trigger and then Trigger Now (see Figure 5-26).

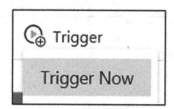

Figure 5-26. *Running an Azure Data factory pipeline*

24) Click Finish.

25) Click the Monitor option to monitor the progress (see Figure 5-27).

Figure 5-27. *Pipeline progress*

26) Once the pipeline has executed successfully, switch to the Azure SQL Data Warehouse query editor to view the tables and data. Let's first see the error records (see Figure 5-28).

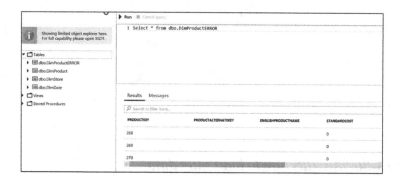

Figure 5-28. *Querying SQL Data Warehouse to check error data*

Let's query the product dimension table (see Figure 5-29).

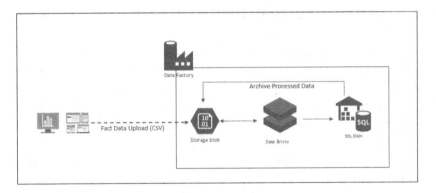

Figure 5-29. *Querying SQL Data Warehouse to verify dimension data*

Let's add sales data to Azure SQL Data Warehouse. In this chapter, we didn't discuss how to delete files from Azure Blob Storage once they're processed successfully. We'll cover that in a later chapter. Figure 5-30 shows the architecture you'll build.

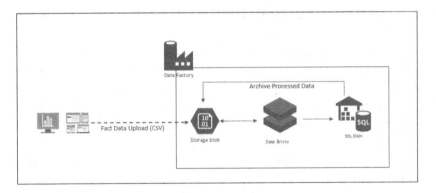

Figure 5-30. *Architecture to load sales data*

1) Switch to the Azure SQL Data Warehouse query
    editor to create a fact table using the following script
    (see Figure 5-31):

```
CREATE TABLE [dbo].[FactStoreSales](
[SalesOrderID] [int] NULL,
[StoreId] [int] NULL,
[OrderDate] [date] NULL,
[SubTotal] [decimal](18, 2) NULL,
[Taxperc] [int] NULL,
[TaxAmt] [decimal](18, 2) NULL,
[Freightperc] [int] NULL,
[Freight] [decimal](18, 2) NULL,
[TotalDue] [decimal](18, 2) NULL,
[SalesOrderDetailID] [int] NULL,
[ProductKey] [bigint] NULL,
[OrderQty] [int] NULL,
[UnitPrice] [decimal](18, 2) NULL,
[UnitPriceDiscount] [decimal](18, 2) NULL,
[LineTotal] [decimal](18, 2) NULL
 )
```

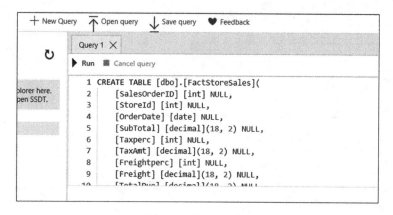

Figure 5-31. *Building the fact table*

213

2) Upload the sales data to Azure Blob Storage (see Figure 5-32).

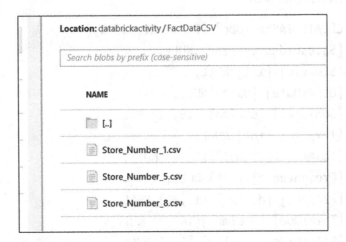

Figure 5-32. *Sales data in CSV format*

3) Figure 5-33 shows the Databricks script that will get executed from Azure Data Factory. Create a notebook (Python) in your Azure Databricks account and put the code there.

Figure 5-33. *Azure Databricks Python code*

4) Switch to the Azure Data Factory Author & Monitor UI.

5) Drag and drop a Notebook activity, as shown in Figure 5-34.

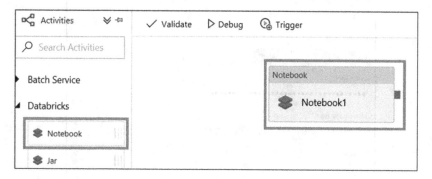

Figure 5-34. *Building the Azure data pipeline*

6) On the General tab, provide a name and description for the activity.

7) On the Azure Databricks tab, create or use the existing Databricks linked service.

8) If you are creating a new Databricks linked activity, provide the name, add a description, select your subscription, provide the Databricks workspace, generate a token if you don't have one, and add the cluster details, as shown in Figure 5-35.

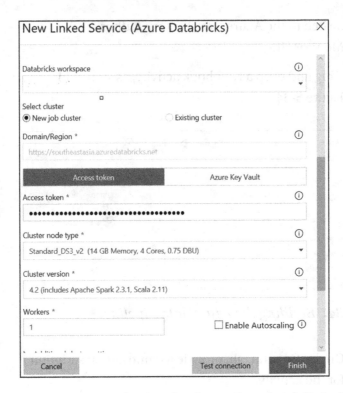

Figure 5-35. *Parameter selection for Azure Databrick linked service*

9)   Click Finish.

10)   On the Settings tab, provide the notebook path, as
      shown in Figure 5-36.

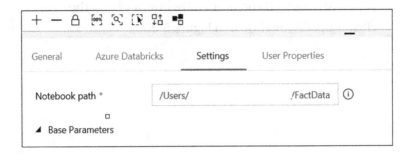

Figure 5-36. *Setting a notebook path*

11) Drag and drop a Copy Data activity and connect it
with the Notebook activity, as shown in Figure 5-37.

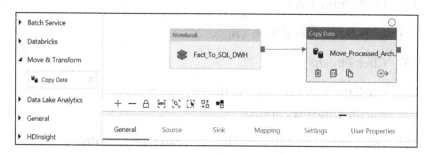

Figure 5-37. *Setting up the Azure Data Factory pipeline*

12) On the Source tab, provide the link to the location of
the raw files (see Figure 5-38).

Figure 5-38. *Setting a connection to Azure Blob Storage*

13) Similarly, provide a link service to Azure Blob Storage where you want to store archive files.

14) Click Publish All.

15) Click Trigger and then Trigger Now.

16) Click Finish.

17) Click the Monitor icon on the left side to monitor the pipeline execution.

18) Once completed successfully, you can query the data in Azure SQL Data Warehouse (see Figure 5-39).

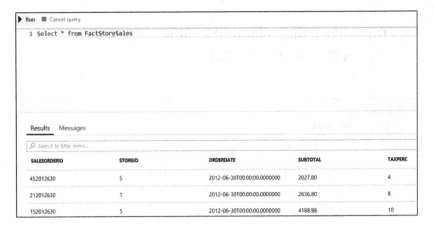

Figure 5-39. *Querying the fact table in SQL Data Warehouse*

19) Click Azure Blob Storage to see the files copied in Azure Blob Storage (see Figure 5-40).

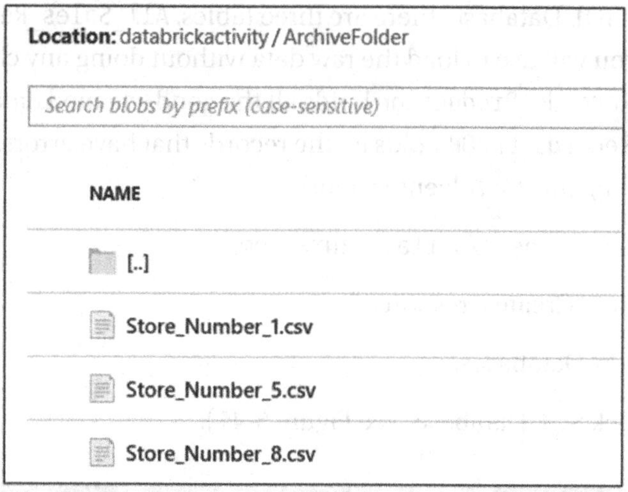

Figure 5-40. *Verifying the file movement*

Stored Procedure

Running a stored procedure is another way to transform data into deeper insights and predictions. The benefit of running a stored procedure is that it provides compute near the data, which means the data doesn't need to travel for processing. You can invoke a Stored Procedure activity to Azure SQL Database, Azure SQL Data Warehouse, and a SQL Server database on-premises or via a virtual machine (VM). In the case of on-premises storage, you need to install the self-hosted integration runtime. Organizations use stored procedures to clean and move data from staging to the production database. This is a classic example of ELT. Since the stored procedure runs on the database server, you'll need to validate whether executing the heavy-lifting job causes any performance issues.

Let's say AdventureWorks wants to evaluate how to transform data using the ELT methodology. In this scenario, assume that it's available in Azure Blob Storage (in CSV format). Using Azure Data Factory, you will move data to Azure SQL Database and then run a stored procedure to clean the data (primarily removing duplicate records).

In Azure SQL Database, there are three tables. `All_Sales_Records_Raw` is the table you will use to load the raw data without doing any cleaning. `All_Sales_Records_Production` holds all the good/cleaned data, and `All_Sales_Records_ERROR` holds all the records that have errors. Let's get started building this for AdventureWorks.

1) Go to `https://portal.azure.com`.

2) Click "Create a resource."

3) Click Databases.

4) Click SQL Database (see Figure 5-41).

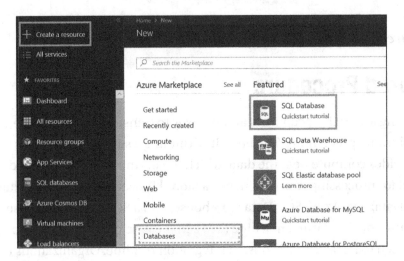

Figure 5-41. *Creating a SQL database*

5) Fill in the following details and click Create to set up the new Azure SQL Server instance (see Figure 5-42).

Figure 5-42. *Inputting values to set up Azure SQL Database*

6)   Let's use SQL Server Management Studio (SSMS) to connect to the Azure SQL server, or you can use the query editor (see Figure 5-43).

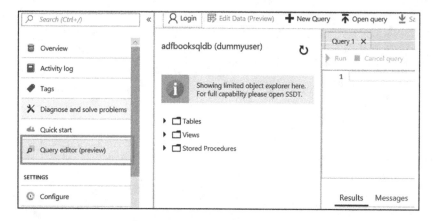

Figure 5-43. *Switching to the query editor*

7) If you plan to use SSMS, please set your machine IP to Azure SQL so that you can access it from your computer (SSMS), as shown in Figure 5-44.

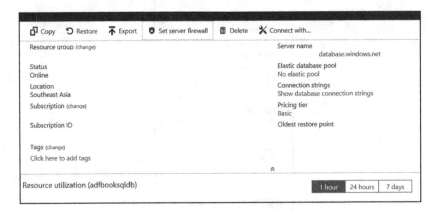

Figure 5-44. *Accessing Azure SQL Server from the client tool*

8) Create the SQL Server table and stored procedure as provided. Figure 5-45 shows the structure after running the table and stored procedure scripts.

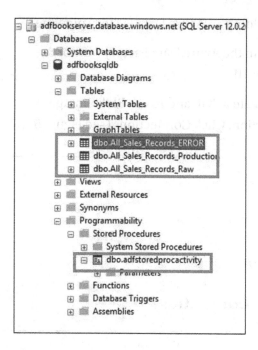

Figure 5-45. *Artifact in Azure SQL Database*

9) Upload the data file (provided) to Azure Blob Storage (see Figure 5-46).

Figure 5-46. *Data file in Azure Blob Storage*

Let's start building an Azure Data Factory pipeline.

1) Switch to the Azure Data Factory Author &
Monitor UI.

2) Let's create a SQL and Azure Blob Storage
connection. Click Connections (see Figure 5-47).

Figure 5-47. *Setting up a connection*

3) Click +New (see Figure 5-48).

Figure 5-48. *Creating new linked services*

4) Select Azure Blob Storage (see Figure 5-49).

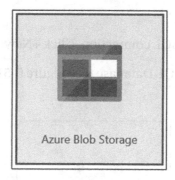

Figure 5-49. *Azure Blob Storage option*

5) Click Continue.

6) Provide information about the storage where you
    uploaded your data file (see Figure 5-50).

Figure 5-50. *Azure Blob Storage linked service options*

7) Click Finish.

8) Let's create a SQL connection. Click +New.

9) Select Azure SQL Database (see Figure 5-51).

Azure SQL Database

Figure 5-51. *Azure SQL Database option*

10) Click Continue.

11) Provide information about the Azure SQL Server
instance created in earlier steps (see Figure 5-52).

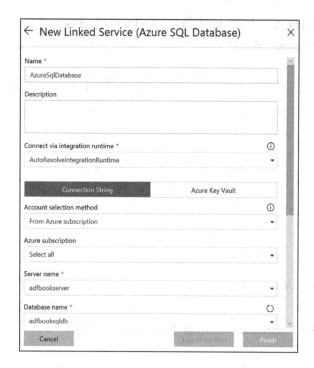

Figure 5-52. *Setting up the Azure SQL Database linked service*

12)   Click Finish.

Finally, you have two connections (see Figure 5-53).

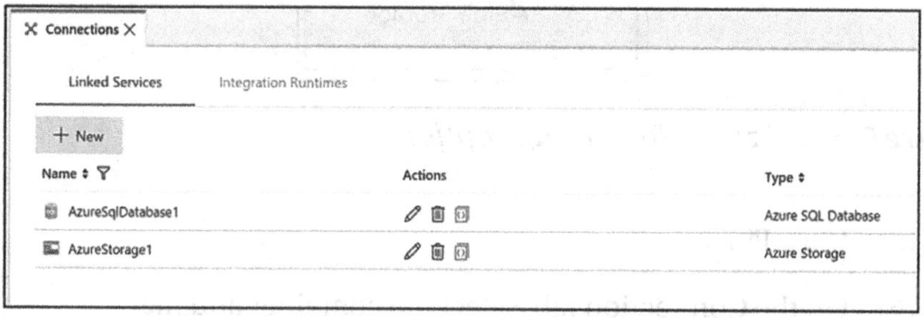

Figure 5-53. *List of available linked service*

13) Let's create datasets. Click + and then Dataset
(see Figure 5-54).

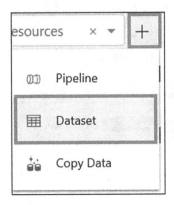

Figure 5-54. *Dataset option*

14) Click Azure Blob Storage (see Figure 5-55).

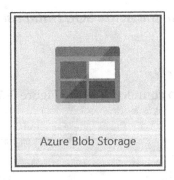

Figure 5-55. *Azure Blob Storage option*

15) Click Finish.

16) On the Connection tab, select the container and file
name that you uploaded earlier (see Figure 5-56).

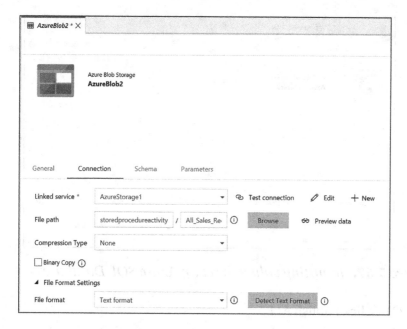

Figure 5-56. Connecting to Azure Blob Storage

17)   Select column names in the first row.

Let's create another dataset on top of the SQL connection created earlier.

18)   Click + and then Dataset.

19)   Select Azure SQL Database.

20)   Click Finish.

21)   On the Connection tab, select the Azure SQL Server
      connection created in the previous step. For Table,
      select All_Sales_Records_Raw (see Figure 5-57).

Figure 5-57. *Inputting values to set up Azure SQL Database*

22) Click Publish ALL.

23) Click + and then Pipeline.

24) Drag and drop the Copy Data activity, as shown in Figure 5-58.

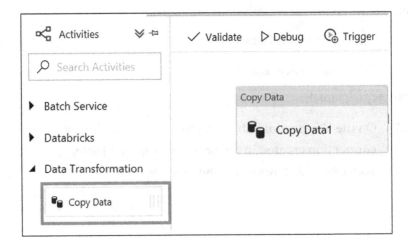

Figure 5-58. *Copy Data activity option*

25) On the Source tab, select the Azure Blob Storage
dataset created earlier (see Figure 5-59).

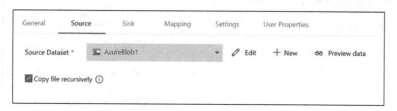

Figure 5-59. *Source selection for the Copy activity*

26) On the Sink tab, select the Azure SQL dataset
created earlier (see Figure 5-60).

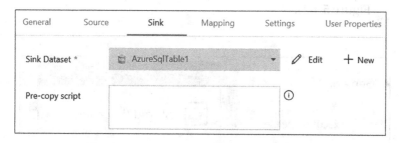

Figure 5-60. *Sink selection for the Copy activity*

27) On the Mapping tab, click Import Schemas. Since
the column names are the same on the source and
target, the mapping is done automatically (see
Figure 5-61).

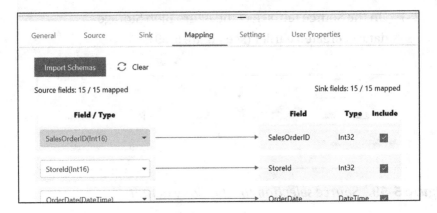

Figure 5-61. *Field mapping*

28) Drag and drop the Stored Procedure activity (see Figure 5-62).

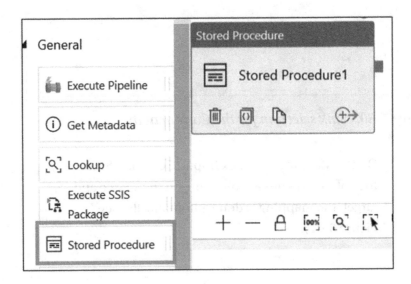

Figure 5-62. *Stored Procedure activity*

29) Select the Copy Data activity, click the "Add activity on:" option, select Success, and then drag the arrow to the Stored Procedure activity. This means run the next process if the current activity runs successfully (see Figure 5-63).

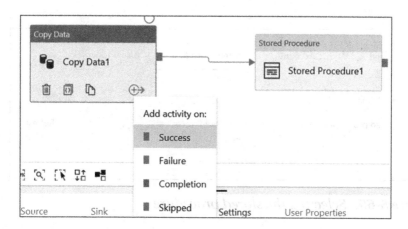

Figure 5-63. *Setting up a link between two activities*

30) Select Stored Procedure (see Figure 5-64).

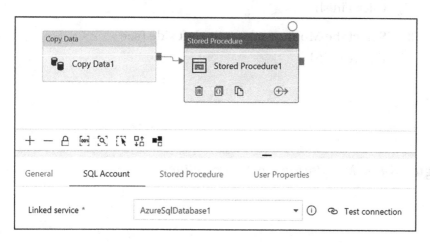

Figure 5-64. *Setting values for the stored procedure*

233

31) On the SQL Account tab, select "Azure SQL Database connection" for "Linked service."

32) On the Stored Procedure tab, select the stored procedure (adfstoredprocactivity) created earlier (see Figure 5-65).

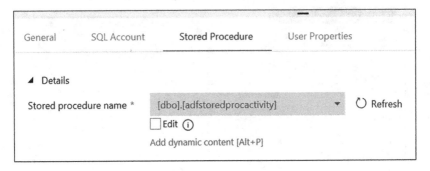

Figure 5-65. *Selecting the stored procedure*

33) Click Publish All.

34) Click Trigger and then Trigger Now.

35) Click Finish.

36) Select the Monitor tab on the left side (see Figure 5-66).

Figure 5-66. *Monitoring the ADF pipeline*

37)   Once pipeline execution happens successfully, query the database (see Figure 5-67).

```
Select top 10 *  from [dbo].[All_Sales_Records_Raw]
Select top 10 *  from [dbo].[All_Sales_Records_Production]
Select * from [dbo].[All_Sales_Records_ERROR]
```

10 %

Results   Messages

	SalesOrderID	StoreId	OrderDate	SubTotal	Taxperc	TaxAmt	Freightperc	Freight	TotalDue	SalesOrderDetailID	PName
1	9	2	2012-06-30	11777	12	1413	1	117	13308	7	Touring-3000 Yellow 44
2	9	2	2012-06-30	11777	12	1413	1	117	13308	8	Racing Socks M
3	10	2	2012-06-30	2901	4	116	0	0	3017	1	Mountain-200 Silver 46
4	10	2	2012-06-30	2901	4	116	0	0	3017	2	Hydration Pack - 70 oz.
5	10	2	2012-06-30	2901	4	116	0	0	3017	3	LL Mountain Frame - Bla
6	11	2	2012-06-30	3244	11	356	1	32	3634	1	Road-250 Black 58
7	11	2	2012-06-30	3244	11	356	1	32	3634	2	Sport-100 Helmet Black
8	11	2	2012-06-30	3244	11	356	1	32	3634	3	Bike Wash - Dissolver

	SalesOrderID	StoreId	OrderDate	SubTotal	Taxperc	TaxAmt	Freightperc	Freight	TotalDue	SalesOrderDetailID	PName
1	1	1	2013-01-03	3022	5	151	0	0	3174	4	Long-Sleeve Logo Jerse
2	1	1	2013-01-04	150	2	3	0	0	153	1	Mountain Tire Tube
3	1	1	2013-01-04	150	2	3	0	0	153	2	LL Mountain Front Whe
4	1	1	2013-01-05	174	5	8	1	1	185	1	Mountain Tire Tube
5	1	1	2013-01-05	174	5	8	1	1	185	2	Sport-100 Helmet Black
6	1	1	2013-01-05	174	5	8	1	1	185	3	Short-Sleeve Classic Jer
7	1	1	2013-01-05	174	5	8	1	1	185	4	Sport-100 Helmet Red
8	1	1	2013-01-06	1303	2	26	1	13	1342	1	Road-650 Red 60

	SalesOrderID	StoreId	OrderDate	SubTotal	Taxperc	TaxAmt	Freightperc	Freight	TotalDue	SalesOrderDetailID	PName	OrderQty
1	1	1	2012-06-30	2524	5	126	1	25	2675	1	HL Fork	5
2	1	5	2012-07-01	7990	9	719	0	0	8709	4	Patch...	1
3	2	1	2012-06-30	2636	8	210	1	26	2874	1	HL M...	3
4	3	1	2012-06-30	5602	6	336	1	56	5994	4	Road-...	1
5	5	8	2012-07-01	3588	12	430	1	35	4055	3	Bike	1

Figure 5-67. *SQL query to validate the transformation*

Custom Activity

So far, you have seen various activities that can be used in Azure Data Factory for data transformation. Why would you need a custom activity?

It is not always the case that you will go with the built-in activities to transform data. There are many scenarios where developers want to add their own logic in a programming language for transformation. For example, you might want to read a document, extract specific information and store it in a database, or call an API to retrieve data and store it or any other customization; these are not built-in tasks. In a nutshell, if Azure Data Factory doesn't support the transformation that you are looking for, then you can use a Custom activity to write your own transformation.

Azure Data Factory uses Azure Batch services to help developers run their own code in any operating system (Windows/Linux). Configuring the scaling feature of Azure Batch services guarantees to provide the scalability that the enterprise wants (see Figure 5-68).

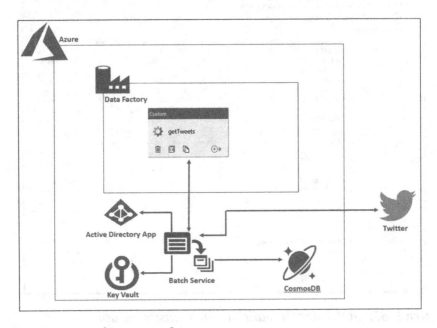

Figure 5-68. *Reference architecture*

Let's set up a Twitter application that retrieves credentials for making API calls to get tweets for a specific tag.

1) Go to `https://apps.twitter.com/`.

2) Click Create New App.

3) Fill out the information (see Figure 5-69).

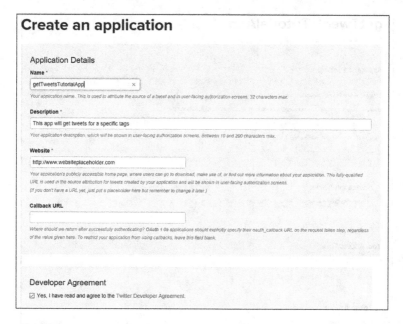

Figure 5-69. *Setting up a Twitter application*

4) Click Create New Application.

5) Once the application is created, go to Keys and Access Tokens (see Figure 5-70).

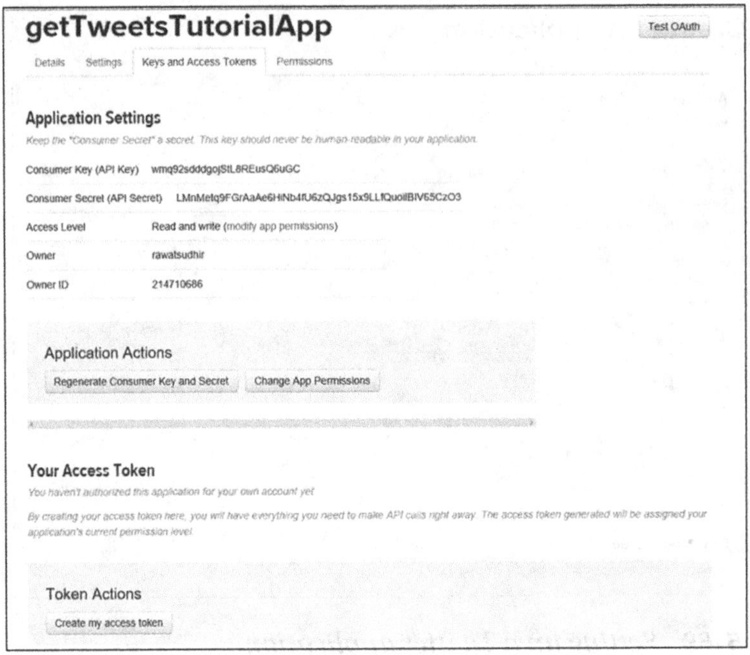

Figure 5-70. *Application settings*

6) Click "Create my access token" and save it to use it in a future step.

Let's set up the Azure Active Directory app to get a token and access Azure Key Vault.

1) Switch to `https://portal.azure.com`.

2) Click Azure Active Directory on the left side.

3) Click "App registrations."

4) Click "New application registration" (see Figure 5-71).

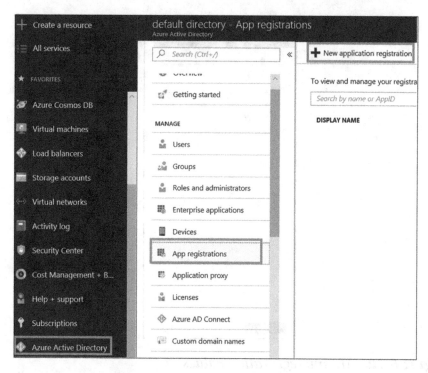

Figure 5-71. *Azure AD app registration option*

5) Provide a name.

6) Select the application type; here select "Web app / API."

7) Provide the sign-on URL. This does not need to be a site that exists (you can put http://test1. adventureworks.com), as shown in Figure 5-72.

Figure 5-72. *AD app registration values*

8) Click Create.

9) Once the app is registered, click it.

10) Click Settings (see Figure 5-73).

Figure 5-73. *Registered app options*

11)   Click Keys in the Password section and then provide
       a description and expiration date. Click Save, and
       it will show the password (see Figure 5-74). Copy it
       into a notepad.

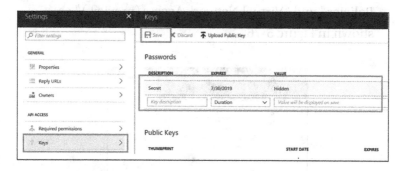

Figure 5-74. *Setting app keys*

Let's set up Azure Key Vault.

1)   Click "Create a resource" and search for *Azure key
       vault* (see Figure 5-75).

Figure 5-75. *Azure Key Vault*

241

2) Select Key Vault and click Create.

3) Enter a name, select your subscription, enter or
   create a resource group, select the right location,
   and leave the defaults for "Pricing tier," "Access
   Policies," and "Virtual Network Access (preview)," as
   shown in Figure 5-76.

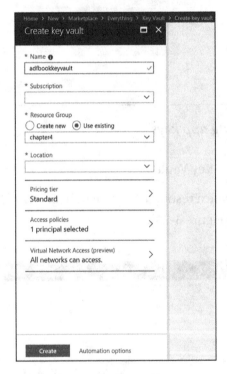

Figure 5-76. *Inputting values to set up Azure Key Vault*

4) Click Create.

Let's set up the Azure Cosmos DB account to store tweets.

1) Click "Create a resource," click Databases, and then
    click Azure Cosmos DB (Figure 5-77).

Figure 5-77. *Setting up Azure Cosmos DB*

2) Provide an ID and the API, select your subscription,
    select or create a resource group, select the right
    location, leave the other settings at the defaults, and
    click Create (see Figure 5-78).

Figure 5-78. *Inputting values to set up Azure Cosmos Database*

3)   At the end, you will see three services added in your
       Azure subscription (see Figure 5-79).

Figure 5-79. *Services set up for this demo so far*

4) Click Azure Cosmos DB Account (created in an
    earlier step).

5) Click Data Explorer and then New Database
    (see Figure 5-80).

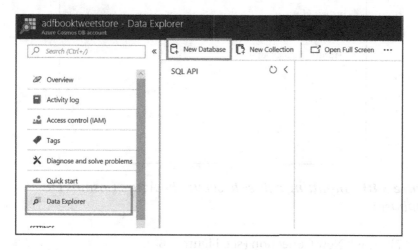

Figure 5-80. *Creating a new Azure Cosmos DB database*

6)   Provide a database ID and click OK (see Figure 5-81).

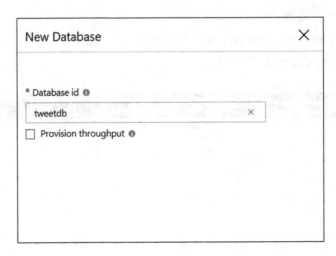

Figure 5-81. *Inputting values to set up the Azure Cosmos DB database*

7)   Click New Collection (see Figure 5-82).

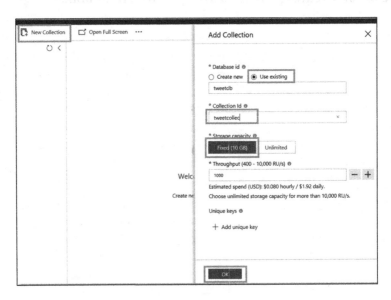

Figure 5-82. *Inputting values to set up a new collection*

8) Select "Use existing" and choose the database ID created in the previous step.

9) Provide the collection ID.

10) Select Fixed (10 GB) as the storage capacity.

11) Click OK.

Let's set up an Azure Batch service.

1) Click "Create a resource."

2) Click Compute.

3) Click Batch Service (see Figure 5-83).

Figure 5-83. *Setting up the Azure Batch service*

4) Provide an account name.

5) Select your subscription.

6) Select or create a new resource group.

7) Select the right location.

8) Select or create a new storage account.

9) Select "Batch service" for "Poll allocation mode" (see Figure 5-84).

Figure 5-84. *Setting up a new Azure Blob Storage account*

10) Click Create.

11) Once the Azure Batch services are set up, you will see services shown in Figure 5-85 on the Azure dashboard (if you choose to pin to dashboard).

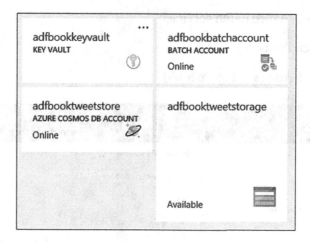

Figure 5-85. *Services set up for this demo*

By default, there is no pool (nodes available for compute) available; hence, let's add a pool. In this demo, let's use a Windows custom image build using a Windows Server 2008 R2 SP1 virtual machine. Make sure to install the software and packages in a virtual machine. Table 5-1 shows the prerequisites.

Table 5-1. *Prerequisites*

Package Name	Description
Python 2.7	Install Python 2.7 from https://www.python.org/downloads/.
install python-pip	Install python-pip to make sure to install the Python packages.
pip install tweepy	Connects to Twitter.
pip install pydocumentdb	Accesses Azure Cosmos DB.
pip install azure-keyvault	Accesses Azure Key Vault.

1) Click "Azure batch service."

2) Click Pools.

3) Click Add (see Figure 5-86).

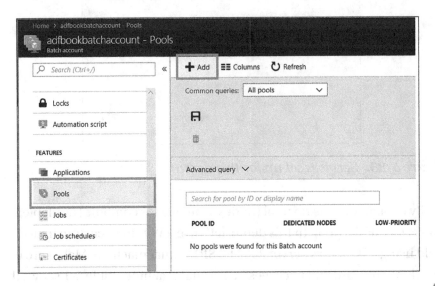

Figure 5-86. *Setting up pools*

4) Add the information in Table 5-2 (see Figure 5-87).

Table 5-2. *Setting Values to Set Up the Pool*

Property	Value
Pool ID	Name of the pool.
Display name	Description (optional).
Image Type	Custom image (Linux/Windows).
Custom VM Image	Select the custom image created earlier.

(continued)

Table 5-2. (*continued*)

Property	Value
Operating System	Windows.
OS Distribution	WindowsServer.
OS version	Microsoft Windows Server 2008 R2 SP1 (latest).
Caching	None.
Container configuration	None.
Metered licenses for rendering	Don't change. You're not doing any rendering for this demo.
Node pricing tier	Standard A1 (1 core, 1.8 GB). This demo is not a compute-extensive job; hence, basic compute works. However, you can go for higher compute.
Mode	Fixed. This service allows you choose the "Auto scale" option, which allows the service to increase/decrease compute based on a formula. This helps the organization not to worry about scaling out and scaling in.
Target dedicated nodes	Set it to 1.
Low priority nodes	0. This option reduces compute cost. Low-priority nodes take advantages of surplus capacity in Azure. You use low-priority nodes when the job consumes less time or for batch processing. The trade-off of using such an option is that the VMs may not be available for allocation or preempted at any time, depending on the available capacity.

(*continued*)

Table 5-2. (*continued*)

Property	Value
Resize Timeout	15 minutes. This is how long the process waits for resizing.
Start task	Disabled. Specify the task that needs to run first when a VM is added to the pool.
Max tasks per node	1. You can specify the maximum number of tasks that can be run on the VM. Be cautious about the VM size you choose.
User accounts	Default.
Task scheduling policy	Pack. This defines how tasks get distributed between VMs in the pool.
Inter-node communication	No.
Application Package	0. In case your application requires packages for it to run successfully.
Certificates	0.
Pool endpoint configuration	Default.
Network configuration	Default. Not required for this demo.
Subnet	Default. Not required for this demo.

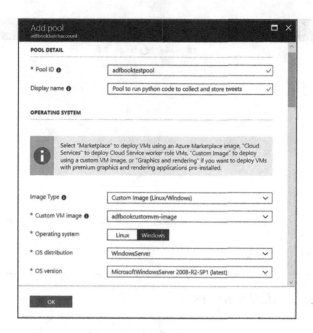

Figure 5-87. *Inputting values to set up a pool*

5) Click OK.

6) Once the pool is created, click Pool (created in the previous step) and then Nodes to make sure a VM is created (see Figure 5-88).

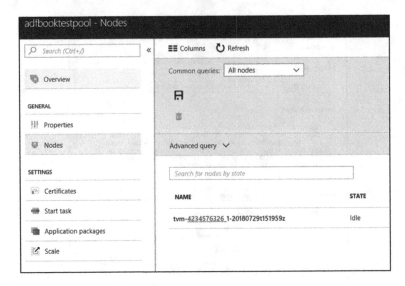

Figure 5-88. *Available nodes*

Let's store credentials on Azure Key Vault and give access to the Azure AD app.

1) Switch to Azure Key Vault.

2) Add all the secrets like the Azure Cosmos DB details and Twitter API details on Azure Key Vault. Switch to the respective services to capture the keys (see Figure 5-89).

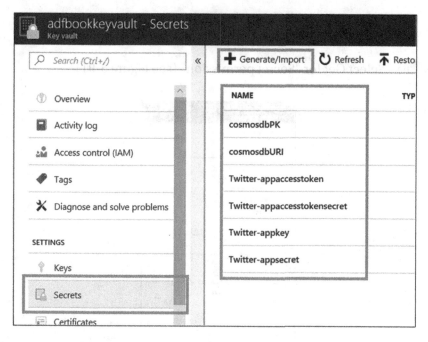

Figure 5-89. *Setting secrets*

3) In Azure Key Vault, click "Access policies."

4) Click +Add New (see Figure 5-90).

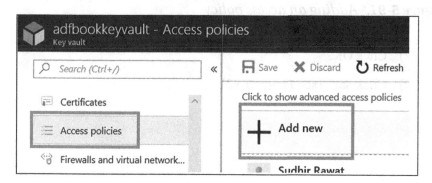

Figure 5-90. *Setting access policies*

5) Select Principal. This is the application registered in Azure Active Directory.

6) Select Get for "Secret permission" (see Figure 5-91).

Figure 5-91. *Adding an access policy*

7) Click OK.

8) Click Save (see Figure 5-92).

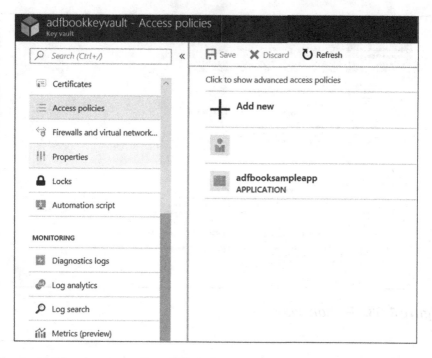

Figure 5-92. *Access policy defined*

Now the environment is set.

Let's look at the Python code. Upload the code to Azure Blob Storage (see Figure 5-93 and Figure 5-94).

```
#Below code is written and tested on Python 2.7
import tweepy
import sys
import pydocumentdb.documents as documents
import pydocumentdb.document_client as document_client
import pydocumentdb.errors as errors
from azure.keyvault import KeyVaultClient, KeyVaultAuthentication
from azure.common.credentials import ServicePrincipalCredentials
class IDisposable:
        def __init__(self, obj):
                self.obj = obj
        def __enter__(self):
                return self.obj # bound to target
        def __exit__(self, exception_type, exception_val, trace):
                self = None
                credentials = None
        def auth_callback(server, resource, scope):
                credentials = ServicePrincipalCredentials(
                client_id = 'XXXXXXXX-XXXX-XXXX-XXXX-XXXXXXXXXXXX', #Azure AD APP Application ID
                secret = 'XXXXXXXXXXXXXXXXXXXXXXXXXXXXXXXXXXXXXXXX', #Secret
                tenant = 'XXXXXXXX-XXXX-XXXX-XXXX-XX-XXXXXXXXXXXX', #Azure AD Directory ID
                resource = "https://vault.azure.net"
                )
        token = credentials.token
        return token['token_type'], token['access_token']

        def insertintoCosmosDB(cdbhost, cdbmasterkey, tweetDate, tweetText):
                tweetmessage = {'tweetDate': str(tweetDate),'id' : str(tweetDate), 'tweetText': tweetText}
                _database_link = 'dbs/tweetdb'
                _collection_link = _database_link + '/colls/tweetcollec'
                with IDisposable(document_client.DocumentClient(cdbhost, {'masterKey': cdbmasterkey} )) as client:
                try:
                        client.CreateDocument(_collection_link, tweetmessage, options=False)
                except errors.DocumentDBError as e:
                        if e.status_code == 409:
                                pass
                        else:
                        raise errors.HTTPFailure(e.status_code)
```

Figure 5-93. *Python code*

```
def main():
# Twitter application key
        client = KeyVaultClient(KeyVaultAuthentication(auth_callback))
        _appkey = client.get_secret("https://XXXX.vault.azure.net/", "Twitter-appkey", "XXXXXXXXXXXXXXXXXXXXXXXX") # KeyVault URL, Secret, Version
        _appsecret= client.get_secret("https://XXXXXX.vault.azure.net/", "Twitter-appsecret", "XXXXXXXXXXXXXXXXXXXXXXXX") # KeyVault URL, Secret, Version
        _appaccesstoken = client.get_secret("https://XXXXXXXXXX.vault.azure.net/", "Twitter-appaccesstoken", "XXXXXXXXXXXXXXXXXXXXXXXX") # KeyVault URL,
        _appaccesstokensecret = client.get_secret("https://XXXXXXXXXX.vault.azure.net/", "Twitter-appaccesstokensecret", "XXXXXXXXXXXXXXXXXXXXXXXX") # ?

        _tweetTag= sys.argv[1] # like Azure
        _tweetReadSince= sys.argv[2] #date from when you want to read tweets like '2018/07/28'
        _RandomId = sys.argv[3] #Azure Data Factory Pipeline ID 'testrun'

# CosmosDB Credential
        _cdbhost = client.get_secret("https://XXXXXXXXX.vault.azure.net/", "cosmosdbURI", "XXXXXXXXXXXXXXXXXXXXXXXX") # KeyVault URL, Secret, Version
        _cdbmasterkey = client.get_secret("https://XXXXXXX.vault.azure.net/", "cosmosdbPK", "XXXXXXXXXXXXXXXXXXXXXXXX") # KeyVault URL, Secret, Version

#hashtag, tweetreadsince, filename includes pipeline id,
        auth = tweepy.OAuthHandler(_appkey.value, _appsecret.value)
        auth.set_access_token(_appaccesstoken.value, _appaccesstokensecret.value)
        tweetapi = tweepy.API(auth,wait_on_rate_limit=True)

        for tweet in tweepy.Cursor(tweetapi.search, q=_tweetTag, lang="en", since=_tweetReadSince).items(15):
                try:
                        if tweet.text.encode('utf-8') != '' :
                                insertintoCosmosDB(_cdbhost.value, _cdbmasterkey.value, tweet.created_at,tweet.text.encode('utf-8'))
                except errors.DocumentDBError as e:
                        if e.status_code == 409:
                                pass
                        else:
                                raise errors.HTTPFailure(e.status_code)
                                print("Error while fetching and storing tweets!!!")
                        break

if __name__ == "__main__":
        main()
```

Figure 5-94. *Python code, continued*

Let's set up Azure Data Factory.

1) Switch to the Azure Data Factory Author &
   Monitor UI.

2) Drag and drop a Custom activity onto the designer
   (see Figure 5-95).

Figure 5-95. *Custom activity*

3) Provide a name and add a description to the activity (see Figure 5-96).

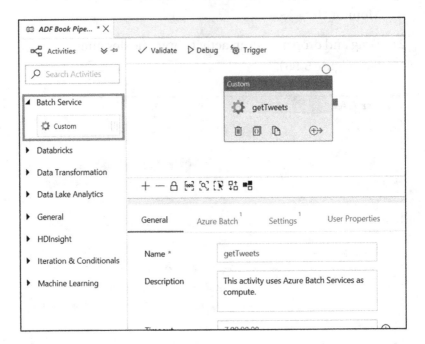

Figure 5-96. *Setting up a Custom activity*

4) On the Azure Batch tab, click +New (see Figure 5-97).

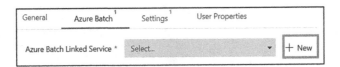

Figure 5-97. *Setting up an Azure Batch linked service*

5) Provide the Azure Batch account details. Retrieve
    all the information from the Azure Batch account
    services (see Figure 5-98).

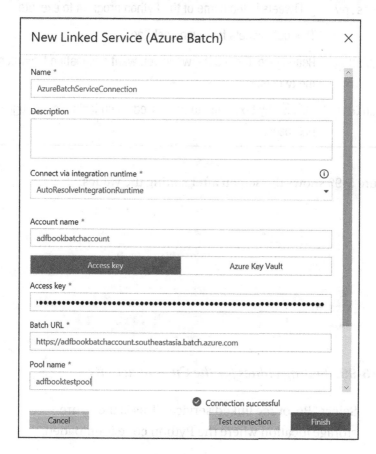

Figure 5-98. Options to set new linked service

6) Click Finish.

7) Click Settings.

8) Provide the command in Command Text Area (see
    Table 5-3).

Table 5-3. *Values for Custom Activity*

Parameter	Description
getTweets.py	getTweets is the name of the Python program to execute.
Azure	This gets tweets for given hash tag.
2018/07/28	Read since. From date, when you want application to capture the tweets.
Todayrunid	This is any text value to be passed when testing or debugging purposes.

Figure 5-99 shows the screen after setting the values.

Figure 5-99. *Setting values for the Custom activity*

9) Select "Resource linked service." This is the Azure storage location where the Python code is uploaded.

10) Select "Folder path." This is the folder location where the Python code is uploaded.

11) Click Publish All.

12) Click Trigger and then Trigger Now.

13) Click Finish.

14) Go to the Monitoring page and wait until the pipeline gets executed successfully (see Figure 5-100).

Figure 5-100. *Monitoring pipeline progress*

Finally, after successful completion, the tweets get stored in Azure Cosmos DB (see Figure 5-101).

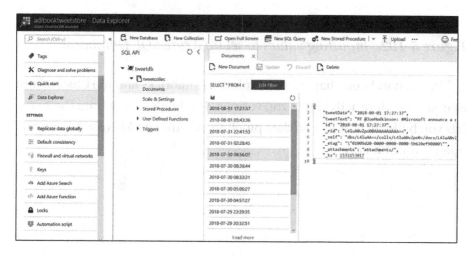

Figure 5-101. *Azure Cosmos DB*

If you encountered any errors, look at the Azure Batch service logs for the specific job to get insight on the type of error encountered (see Figure 5-102).

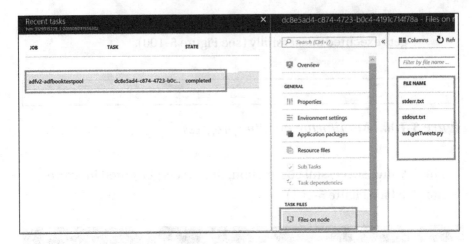

Figure 5-102. *Inputting values to set up Azure SQL Database*

In this hands-on chapter, you explored Databricks and the Custom and Stored Procedure activities to run various workloads. Azure Data Factory lets you build an end-to-end data pipeline, whether on Microsoft or on an open source platform.

CHAPTER 6

Managing Flow

In previous chapters, you focused on the Azure Data Factory features and learned how to build an end-to-end pipeline. The focus of this chapter will be how to set up a pipeline flow and why it's important for any organization.

Why Managing Flow Is Important

So far, you can build an Azure Data Factory pipeline and run it. This chapter will discuss expressions, functions, and activities to control the data flow in an ADF pipeline. Why do you need to manage the flow? An SSIS developer knows the importance of control flow; however, if you are new to this world, then let's look at an example. As a data developer, you build an ADF pipeline to move data from an on-premises SQL Server instance to an Azure SQL Database instance. However, you are asked to move five tables now and six tables later. So, you will create one pipeline and change it later. This will continue as many times as the organization needs data for certain tables. Another example could be you have been asked to move delta/incremental data. This is not a straightforward flow. You need to tweak the ADF pipeline without changing the existing pipeline and redeploying, which may cause errors. That's where you need some mechanism to manage the ADF pipeline from the outside. This means you need to control the application flow from a configuration file that resides outside of the application.

© Sudhir Rawat and Abhishek Narain 2019
S. Rawat and A. Narain, *Understanding Azure Data Factory*,
https://doi.org/10.1007/978-1-4842-4122-6_6

Azure Data Factory provides various activities to manage the pipeline flow. Let's get started with some action.

Expressions

Programming languages need to be able to get values during runtime to decide on the code flow. In Azure Data Factory, when the pipeline executes, you can capture parameter values or system variables to decide on the flow of the data. There are various system variables and functions to help achieve this. You can write an expression and evaluate conditions. Figure 6-1 lists the system variables provided in Azure Data Factory.

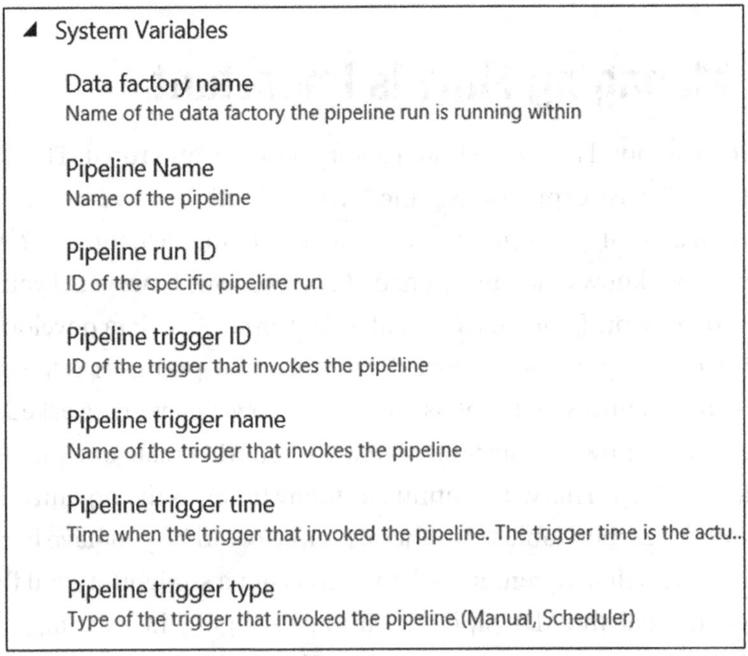

◢ System Variables

Data factory name
Name of the data factory the pipeline run is running within

Pipeline Name
Name of the pipeline

Pipeline run ID
ID of the specific pipeline run

Pipeline trigger ID
ID of the trigger that invokes the pipeline

Pipeline trigger name
Name of the trigger that invokes the pipeline

Pipeline trigger time
Time when the trigger that invoked the pipeline. The trigger time is the actu..

Pipeline trigger type
Type of the trigger that invoked the pipeline (Manual, Scheduler)

Figure 6-1. *System variables*

Functions

There are many functions provided in Azure Data Factory to be used in an expression. For example, there are various types of functions that developers can use to get a value, to check whether a dictionary contains a key, to get a string representation of a data URI, to get an index of a value in a string, to concatenate strings, and so on. Figure 6-2 shows the different types of functions available in Azure Data Factory.

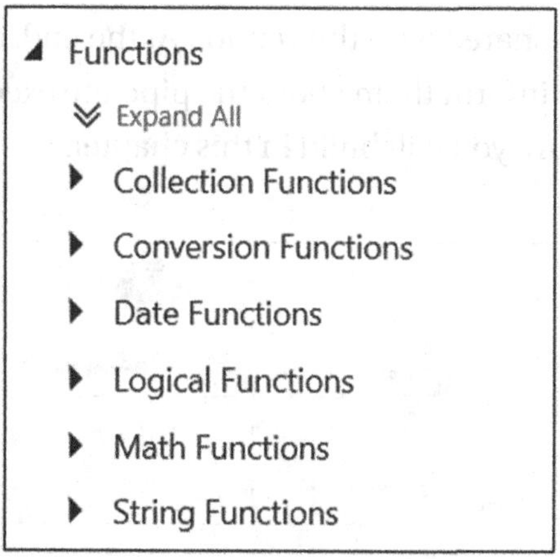

```
▲  Functions
   ⯆  Expand All
   ▶  Collection Functions
   ▶  Conversion Functions
   ▶  Date Functions
   ▶  Logical Functions
   ▶  Math Functions
   ▶  String Functions
```

Figure 6-2. *Functions*

Activities

In all programing languages there are ways to control the code flow such as for loops, if and until statements, and so on. These all help to decide which part of the code needs to be executed. In Azure Data Factory, the control flow activities help to set the direction of the data pipeline execution. For example, the if condition activity provides a way to decide which activity needs to be executed based on a condition.

Let's Build the Flow

Let's build a solution for AdventureWorks to understand how to use the features discussed.

AdventureWorks wants to share increment/delta data with a vendor. The data is stored in different tables of Azure SQL Database. Assume that the data is getting stored on a daily basis. At first, you'll capture all the data and store it in Azure Blob Storage. Then each subsequent day, you need to capture only the delta data from different tables and store it in Azure Blob Storage. This blob is shared with the vendor. At the end, an e-mail is sent to the administrator to inform them about the pipeline execution. Figure 6-3 shows the architecture you will build in this chapter.

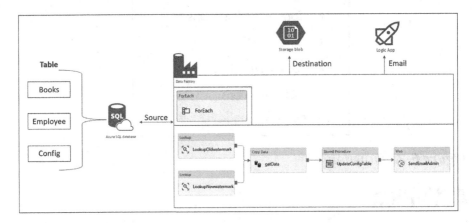

Figure 6-3. *Azure Data Factory pipeline design for delta data loading*

Let's start building this architecture.

Build the Source Database

Here are the steps:

1) Go to https://portal.azure.com.

2) Click "Create a resource."

3) Click Databases.

4) Click SQL Database (see Figure 6-4).

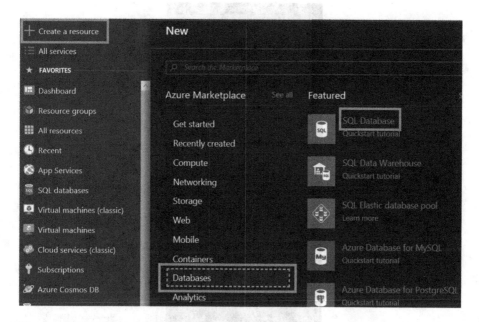

Figure 6-4. *Selecting SQL Database*

5) Use ADFControlFlow for "Database name."

6) Select the subscription where you want to deploy Azure SQL Server.

7) Create or select a resource group.

8) Select "Blank database" for "Select source."

9) For Server, either create a new server or select an existing server.

10) Select "Not now" for "Want to use SQL elastic pool."

11) Select the needed pricing tier.

12) Select the default or provide a Collation value.

13) Click Create (see Figure 6-5).

Figure 6-5. SQL Database setup information

14) Once Azure SQL Server is set up, click "Query editor (preview)," as shown in Figure 6-6, or if you are familiar with SQL Server Management Studio, then execute all scripts there.

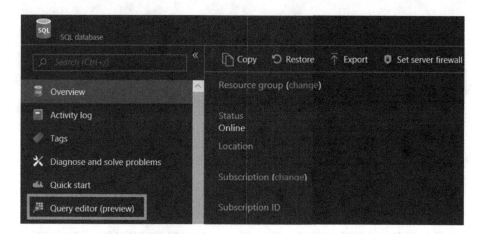

Figure 6-6. *SQL query editor*

15) Click Login.

16) Select "SQL server authentication" for "Authorization type."

17) Provide a login and a password.

18) Click OK (see Figure 6-7).

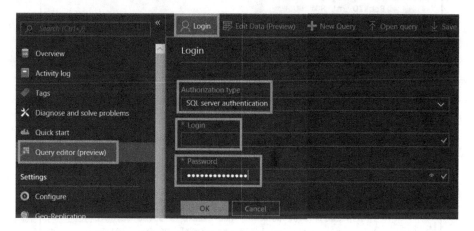

Figure 6-7. *SQL query editor login screen*

19) Run the scripts shown in Figure 6-8, Figure 6-9,
Figure 6-10, and Figure 6-11 one by one.

```
--Create Table to store employee information

CREATE TABLE Employee
        (EmpID INT NOT NULL ,
        EmpName VARCHAR(50) NOT NULL,
        EmpDesignation VARCHAR(50) NULL,
        EmpDepartment VARCHAR(50) NULL,
        EmpJoining DATETIME NULL,
    RecordModifiedDate DATETIME NULL
    CONSTRAINT [PK_Employee] PRIMARY KEY CLUSTERED (EmpID)
)
GO

--Insert records in employee table

INSERT INTO Employee (EmpID, EmpName, EmpDesignation, EmpDepartment, EmpJoining,RecordModifiedDate)
VALUES
(1, 'Abhishek', 'Program Manager', 'PG', GETDATE(),GETDATE() ),
(2, 'Sudhir', 'Senior Software Engineer', 'CSE-CTE',GETDATE(),GETDATE()),
(3, 'Gandhali', 'Software Eng Manager', 'CSE- CTE',GETDATE(),GETDATE()),
(4, 'Shweta', 'Software Eng Manager', 'CSE-CTE', GETDATE(),GETDATE()),
(5, 'Mani', 'Senior Software Eng', 'CSE-EE', GETDATE(),GETDATE())
GO
```

Figure 6-8. *SQL script for table creation and data insertion*

```
--Create book table to store book information

CREATE TABLE [dbo].[Books](
        BookID int NOT NULL,
        BookName varchar(50) NULL,
        BookCategory varchar(50) NULL,
        BookPrice numeric(18, 2) NULL,
        RecordModifiedDate DATETIME NULL
        PRIMARY KEY CLUSTERED ( BookID ASC )
) ON [PRIMARY]
GO

--Insert records in books table

INSERT INTO dbo.Books
        (BookID, BookName, BookCategory, BookPrice,RecordModifiedDate)
VALUES
        (1,'Microsoft Azure', 'Computers', 125.6,GETDATE()),
        (2,'Advanced AI', 'Statistics', 172.56,GETDATE()),
        (3,'Asp.Net 4 Blue Book', 'Programming', 56.00,GETDATE()),
        (4,'Visual Studio Code', 'Programming', 99.99,GETDATE())
GO
```

Figure 6-9. *SQL script for table creation and data insertion, continued*

272

```
--Create a configuration table

CREATE TABLE [dbo].[config](
    [Table_Schema] [varchar](200) NULL,
    [Table_Name] [varchar](200) NULL,
    [WatermarkValue] [datetime] NULL
) ON [PRIMARY]
GO


-- Insert records in config table
INSERT INTO [dbo].[config]
        ([Table_Schema]
        ,[Table_Name])
    VALUES
        ('dbo','Books'),
    ('dbo','Employee')
GO
```

Figure 6-10. *SQL script for table creation and data insertion, continued*

```
--Create stored procedure to update configuration table

CREATE PROCEDURE spupdatewatermark @RecordModifiedtime datetime, @TableName varchar(50)
AS
BEGIN
        UPDATE config
        SET [WatermarkValue] = @RecordModifiedtime
    WHERE [Table_Name] = @TableName
END
```

Figure 6-11. *SQL script for stored procedure creation*

Build Azure Blob Storage as the Destination

Follow these steps:

1) Switch to https://portal.azure.com.

2) Click "Create a resource."

3)   Click Storage.

4)   Click "Storage account - blob, file, table, queue" (see Figure 6-12).

Figure 6-12.   *Azure Blob Storage service selection*

5)   Provide all the requested information to set up Azure Blob Storage and click Create (see Figure 6-13).

Figure 6-13. *Azure Blob Storage selection*

6) Once the Azure Blob Storage setup is done, click "Storage Explorer (preview)."

7) Right-click Blob Containers and click Create Blob Container (see Figure 6-14).

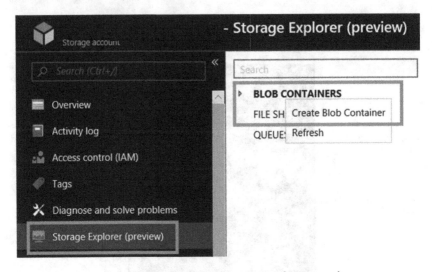

Figure 6-14. *Access Azure Storage Explorer (preview)*

8) Provide a name and public access level (see Figure 6-15).

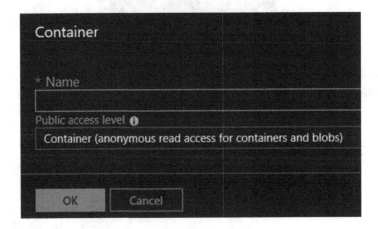

Figure 6-15. *Container name and access level screen*

9) Click OK.

Build the Azure Logic App

Follow these steps:

1) Switch to https://portal.azure.com.

2) Click "Create a resource," then Integration, and then Logic App (see Figure 6-16).

Figure 6-16. *Azure Logic App service selection*

3) Provide a name, select your subscription, create or
   select a resource group, select the right location,
   enable or disable Log Analytics, and click Create
   (see Figure 6-17).

Figure 6-17. *Azure Logic App service creation*

4) Once the Azure Logic App is created, click Edit (see
   Figure 6-18).

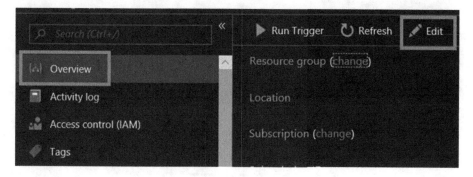

Figure 6-18. *Clicking Edit*

5) Select "When a HTTP request is received" from the
   Logic Apps Designer (see Figure 6-19).

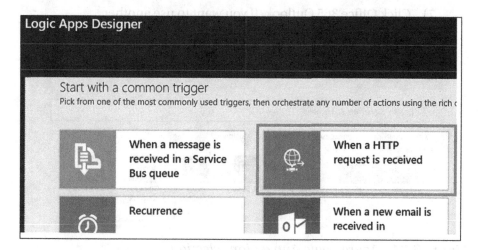

Figure 6-19. *Azure Logic App trigger selection*

6)   Click "+ New step" (see Figure 6-20).

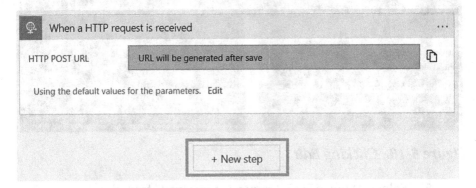

Figure 6-20. *Azure Logic Apps Designer*

7)   Click Office 365 Outlook. If you want to use another e-mail provider like Gmail, you can (see Figure 6-21).

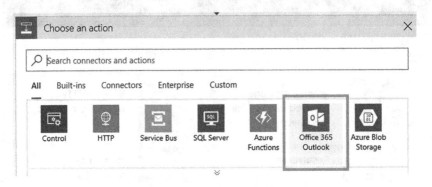

Figure 6-21. *Azure Logic App action selection*

8)   Click "Send an email" (see Figure 6-22).

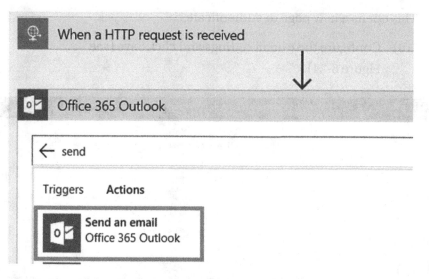

Figure 6-22. *Azure Logic App action configuration*

9) Click "Sign in" (see Figure 6-23).

Figure 6-23. *Azure Logic App Outlook authentication link*

This opens a new page to authenticate.

10) Configure the e-mail settings and click Save (see
     Figure 6-24).

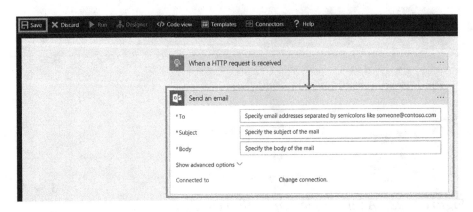

Figure 6-24. *Azure Logic App Office 365 Outlook e-mail*
configuration

11) Once the Logic App is saved, you can view the HTTP
     POST URL (see Figure 6-25).

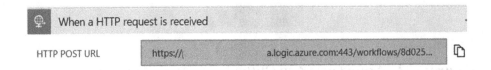

Figure 6-25. *Azure Logic App HTTP POST URL*

12) Add the value shown in Figure 6-26 in Request Body
     JSON Schema.

```json
{
    "type": "object",
    "properties": {
        "pipeline_run_time": {
            "type": "string"
        },
        "data_factory_name": {
            "type": "string"
        }
    }
}
```

Figure 6-26. *JSON schema*

13) The screen will look like Figure 6-27 after entering the value.

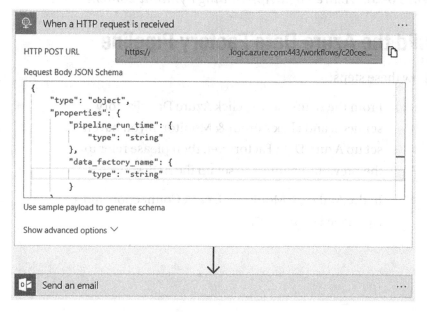

Figure 6-27. *Azure Logic App HTTP request body configuration*

14) In the "Send an email" activity, add a custom
message adding dynamic content, as shown in
Figure 6-28.

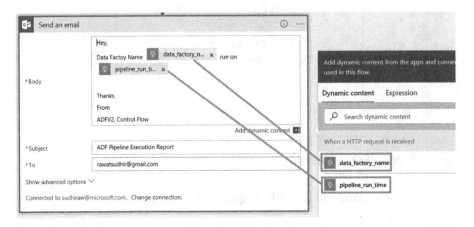

Figure 6-28. *Azure Logic App adding dynamic content*

Build the Azure Data Factory Pipeline

Follow these steps:

1) From the Azure portal, click Azure Data Factory
services, and click Author & Monitor. If you haven't
set up Azure Data Factory yet, then please refer to
the previous chapters to set up the ADF service.

2) In the Author & Monitor UI, click Connection and +
New (see Figure 6-29).

Figure 6-29. *Azure Data Factory new connection*

3) Create two connections: one for Azure SQL
    Database (the service created earlier) and another
    for Azure Blob Storage (the service created earlier).
    Please refer to Chapter 5 if you are not sure how
    to create connections. Once you have created the
    connections, the screen will look like Figure 6-30.

+ New		
Name ⬍ ▽	Actions	Type ⬍
🖼 AzureStorage1	✐ 🗑 ⧉	Azure Storage
🗄 cfsourcesql	✐ 🗑 ⧉	Azure SQL Database

Figure 6-30. *Azure Data Factory connections*

4)   Let's create datasets. Click + and then Dataset (see Figure 6-31).

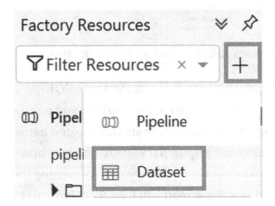

Figure 6-31. *Azure Data Factory dataset option*

5)   Select Azure SQL Database and click Finish (see Figure 6-32).

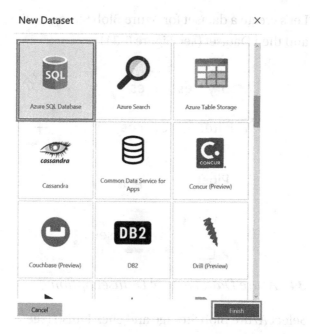

Figure 6-32. *Azure Data Factory Azure SQL Database selection*

6) On the General tab, provide a name and add a
description.

7) On the Connection tab, select the connection you
created earlier for "Linked service." Don't choose
any value for Table (see Figure 6-33).

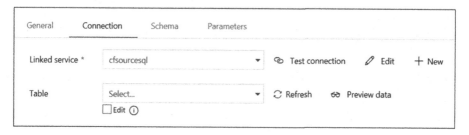

Figure 6-33. *Azure Data Factory Azure SQL database*
configuration

8) Let's create a dataset for Azure Blob Storage. Click + and then Dataset (see Figure 6-34).

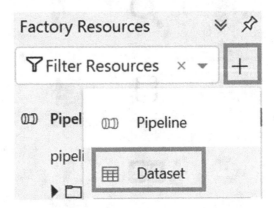

Figure 6-34. *Azure Data Factory Dataset option*

9) Select Azure Blob Storage and click Finish (see Figure 6-35).

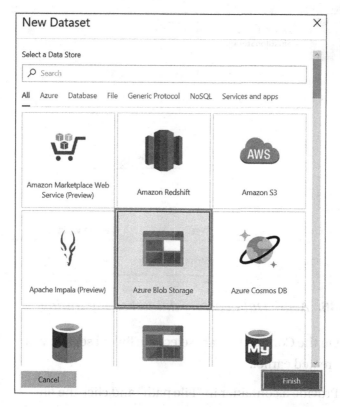

Figure 6-35. *Azure Data Factory Azure Blob Storage dataset selection*

10) On the General tab, provide a name and add a description.

11) On the Parameters tab, click New and provide a variable name for Name, select String for Type, and leave Default Value blank (see Figure 6-36).

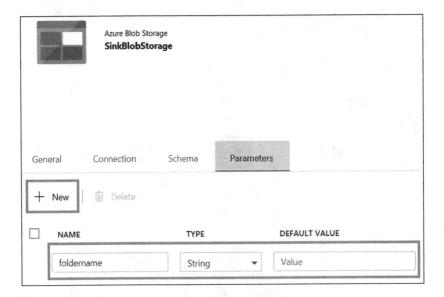

Figure 6-36. *Azure Data Factory dataset configuration*

12) On the Connection tab, select the linked service you created earlier.

13) Provide a container in "File path" and click the file name area to add the parameter.

14) Select the parameter name and click Finish (see Figure 6-37).

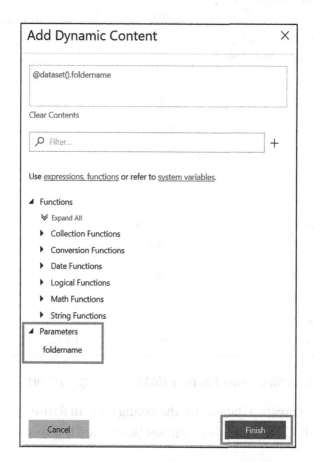

Figure 6-37. *Azure Data Factory parameter listing*

15) Select "Text format" for "File format." The screen will look like Figure 6-38.

Azure Blob Storage
SinkBlobStorage

General   Connection   Schema   Parameters

Linked service *	AzureStorage1 ▼	🔗 Test connection ✏ Edi
File path	sinkblobstorage / @dataset().foldername	Browse 👁 Previe
Compression Type	None ▼	

☐ Binary Copy ⓘ

▲ File Format Settings

File format	Text format ▼ ⓘ	Detect Text Format ⓘ

Figure 6-38. *Azure Data Factory dataset configuration*

16) Let's create a dataset for the config table in Azure
     SQL. Click + and then Dataset (see Figure 6-39).

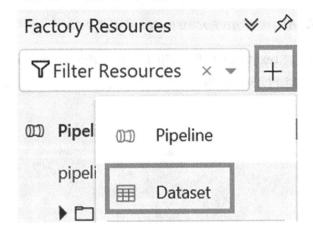

Figure 6-39. *Azure Data Factory Dataset option*

17) On the General tab, provide a name and add a description.

18) On the Connection tab, select the Azure SQL connection created earlier. Provide [dbo].[config] for Table (see Figure 6-40).

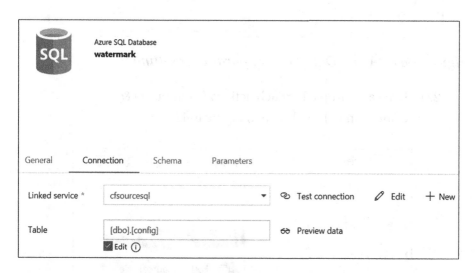

Figure 6-40. *Azure Data Factory dataset configuration*

19) Once the dataset is set up, let's create a pipeline. Click + and then Pipeline.

20) On the General tab, provide a name and add a description.

21) On the Parameters tab, click + New and create a new parameter, as shown in Figure 6-41.

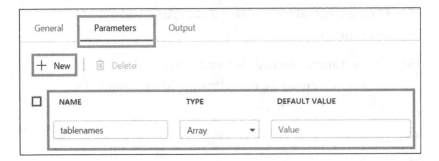

Figure 6-41. *Azure Data Factory parameter setting*

22)   Drag and drop a ForEach activity (in Iteration &
Conditionals), as shown in Figure 6-42.

Figure 6-42. *Adding a ForEach activity*

23) On the General tab, provide a name and add a description.

24) In Settings, provide "@pipeline().parameters. tablenames" for Items (see Figure 6-43).

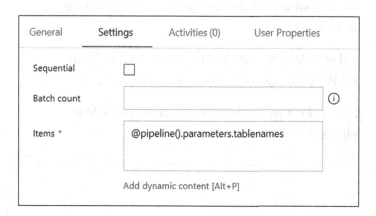

Figure 6-43. *Azure Data Factory configuring activity*

25) Under Activities (0), click "Add activity."

26) Drag and drop the Lookup activity (see Figure 6-44).

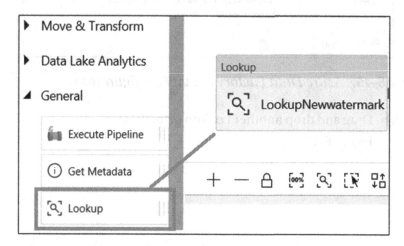

Figure 6-44. *Adding a Lookup activity*

27) On the General tab, provide a name
    (LookupNewwatermark) and add a description.

28) In Settings, select "Azure SQL dataset" for Source
    Dataset, and select Query for Use Query. Provide
    the following code in the Query area to get a new
    watermark:

    ```
    select MAX(@{item().WaterMark_Column}) as
    NewWatermarkvalue from   @{item().TABLE_NAME}
    ```

29) Select "First row only." The screen will look like
    Figure 6-45.

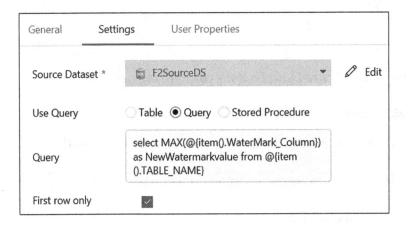

Figure 6-45. *Azure Data Factory activity configuration*

30) Drag and drop another Lookup activity (see
    Figure 6-46).

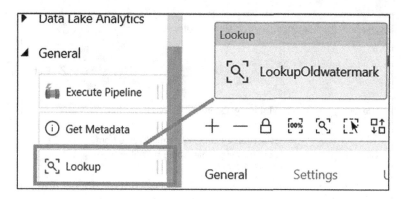

Figure 6-46. *Adding another Lookup activity*

31) On the General tab, provide a name (LookupOldwatermark) and add a description. Let's use the default values for the rest of the properties.

32) On the Settings tab, select the "watermark" dataset for Source Dataset.

33) Select Query for Use Query.

34) Provide the following query in the Query area:

```
select Table_Name, WatermarkValue from Config where
Table_Name = '@{item().TABLE_NAME}'
```

35) Select "First row only." The screen will look like Figure 6-47.

Figure 6-47. Azure Data Factory activity configuration

36) Drag and drop the Copy Data activity (in Move & Transform). Connect both previous activities to the Copy Data activity (see Figure 6-48).

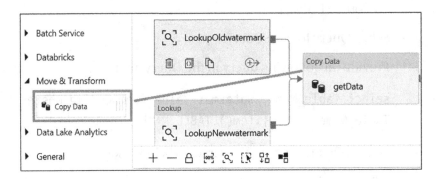

Figure 6-48. Adding a Copy Data activity

37) On the General tab, provide a name (getData) and add a description. Let's use the default values for the rest of the properties.

38) On the Source tab, select "Azure SQL dataset" for Source Dataset. Select Query for Use Query.

39) Provide the following query for Query:

```
select * from @{item().TABLE_NAME} where @{item().
WaterMark_Column} > '@{activity('LookupOldwatermark').
output.firstRow.WatermarkValue}' and @{item().
WaterMark_Column} <= '@{activity('LookupNewwatermark').
output.firstRow.NewWatermarkvalue}'
```

The screen will look like Figure 6-49.

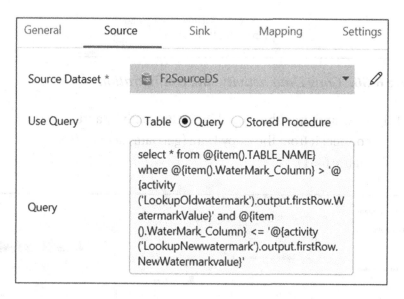

Figure 6-49. Copy Data activity source configuration

40) On the Sink tab, select Azure Blob Storage for Sink Dataset.

41) Provide the following for the folder name:

```
@CONCAT(item().TABLE_NAME, pipeline().RunId, '.txt')
```

The screen will look like Figure 6-50.

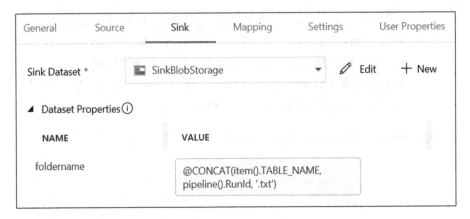

Figure 6-50. *Copy Data activity sink configuration*

42) Drag and drop the Stored Procedure activity and connect it from the Copy Data (getData) activity (see Figure 6-51).

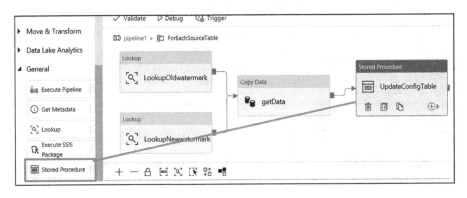

Figure 6-51. *Stored Procedure activity*

43) On the General tab, provide a name (UpdateConfigTable) and add a description. Let's use the default values for rest of the properties.

44) Under SQL Account, select "Azure SQL connection" for "Linked service" (see Figure 6-52).

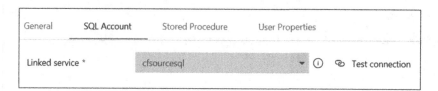

Figure 6-52. *Stored Procedure activity configuration*

45) Provide "[dbo].[spupdatewatermark]" for "Stored procedure name."

46) Click + New for "Stored procedure parameters." Create the parameters listed in Table 6-1.

Table 6-1. *Azure Data Factory Parameter Configuration*

Name	Type	Value
RecordModifiedtime	DateTime	@{activity('LookupNewwatermark').output.firstRow.NewWatermarkvalue}
TableName	String	@{activity('LookupOldwatermark').output.firstRow.Table_Name}

47) After creating the parameters, the screen will look like Figure 6-53.

General	SQL Account	Stored Procedure	User Properties

▲ Details

Stored procedure name *   [dbo].[spupdatewatermark]

☑ Edit ⓘ

Import parameter

Stored procedure parameters ⓘ

➕ New   🗑 Delete

	NAME	TYPE	VALUE
	RecordModifiedtime	DateTime	@{activity('LookupNewwatermark').output.firstRow.NewWatermarkvalue}
	TableName	String	@{activity('LookupOldwatermark').output.firstRow.Table_Name}

***Figure 6-53.** Stored Procedure activity parameter configuration*

48) Drag and drop the Web activity and connect it to the Stored Procedure (UpdateConfigTable) activity (see Figure 6-54).

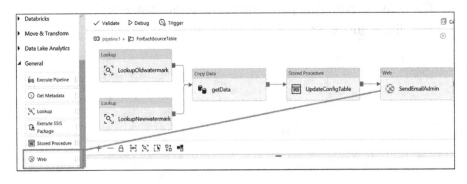

***Figure 6-54.** Stored Procedure activity parameter*

49) On the General tab, provide a name (UpdateConfigTable) and add a description. Let's use the default values for rest of the properties.

50) On the Settings tab, provide the URL (copied from the Azure logic apps).

51) Select POST for Method.

52) Add the following value in Body:

```
{
        pipeline_run_time: @{pipeline().TriggerTime},
        data_factory_name:@{pipeline().DataFactory}
}
```

The screen will look like Figure 6-55.

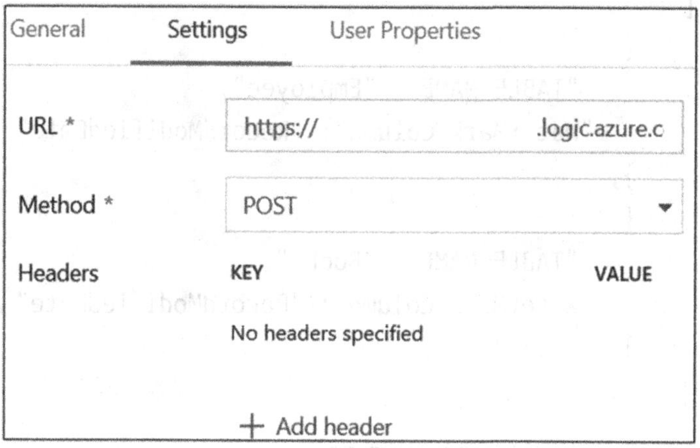

General	Settings	User Properties
URL *	https://	.logic.azure.c
Method *	POST	▼
Headers	KEY	VALUE
	No headers specified	
	+ Add header	

Figure 6-55. *Azure Data Factory web activity configuration*

53)   The final pipeline will look like Figure 6-56.

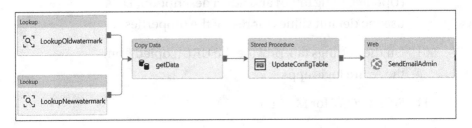

Figure 6-56.   *Azure Data Factory pipeline*

54)   Click Publish All.

55)   Click Trigger and then "Trigger now."

56)   Provide the following value for the tablenames parameter:

```
[
    {
        "TABLE_NAME": "Employee",
        "WaterMark_Column": "RecordModifiedDate"
    },
    {
        "TABLE_NAME": "Books",
        "WaterMark_Column": "RecordModifiedDate"
    }
]
```

The screen will look like Figure 6-57.

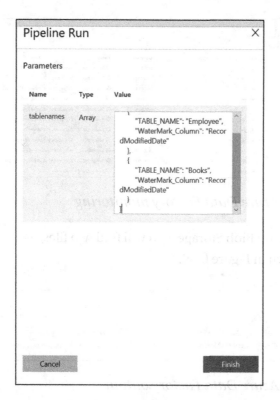

Figure 6-57. *Azure Data Factory parameter passing*

57) Click Finish.

58) Click Monitor and click to drill down to see each activity run. All activity except the main activity (ForEachSourceTable) will run twice because you passed two tables to load data (see Figure 6-58).

Activity Runs

Pipeline Run ID a85b   443de5

All   Succeeded   In Progress   Failed   Cancelled

Activity Name	Activity Type	Actions	Run Start	Duration	Status	Integration Runtime	User Properties	Run
SendEmailAdmin	WebActivity	⊡ ⊡		00:00:01	✓ Succeeded	Unknown		674
SendEmailAdmin	WebActivity	⊡ ⊡		00:00:01	✓ Succeeded	Unknown		bf9c
UpdateConfigTable	SqlServerStoredProcec	⊡ ⊡		00:00:04	✓ Succeeded	DefaultIntegrationRuntime (Southeast Asia)		d5d
UpdateConfigTable	SqlServerStoredProcec	⊡ ⊡		00:00:05	✓ Succeeded	DefaultIntegrationRuntime (Southeast Asia)		2a8
getData	Copy	⊡ ⊡ ∞		00:00:16	✓ Succeeded	DefaultIntegrationRuntime (Southeast Asia)		3f5
getData	Copy	⊡ ⊡ ∞		00:00:16	✓ Succeeded	DefaultIntegrationRuntime (Southeast Asia)		fde
LookupNewwatermark	Lookup	⊡ ⊡		00:00:17	✓ Succeeded	DefaultIntegrationRuntime (Southeast Asia)		cf37
LookupOldwatermark	Lookup	⊡ ⊡		00:00:16	✓ Succeeded	DefaultIntegrationRuntime (Southeast Asia)		94a
LookupOldwatermark	Lookup	⊡ ⊡		00:00:17	✓ Succeeded	DefaultIntegrationRuntime (Southeast Asia)		cf84
LookupNewwatermark	Lookup	⊡ ⊡		00:00:17	✓ Succeeded	DefaultIntegrationRuntime (Southeast Asia)		dd0
ForEachSourceTable	ForEach	⊡ ⊡		00:00:55	✓ Succeeded	Unknown		d33

Figure 6-58. *Azure Data Factory monitoring*

59)   In Azure Blob Storage, you will find two files, as
      shown in Figure 6-59.

← → ⌄ ↑   sinkblobstorage

Name	^	Last Modified	Blob Type	Content Type	Size	Lease State
⧠ Booksa85bf2b5-5168-4486-9aec-8e5436443de5.txt			Block Blob	application/octet-stream	262 B	
⧠ Employeea85bf2b5-5168-4486-9aec-8e5436443de5.txt			Block Blob	application/octet-stream	484 B	

Figure 6-59. *Azure Data Factory output*

60)   Open the files to look at the data (see Figure 6-60).

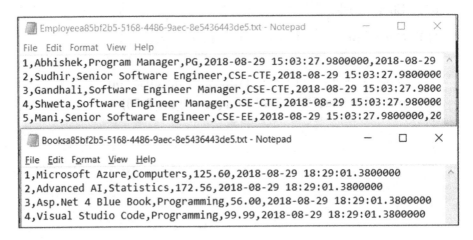

📓 Employeea85bf2b5-5168-4486-9aec-8e5436443de5.txt - Notepad   —   □   ✕

File   Edit   Format   View   Help

```
1,Abhishek,Program Manager,PG,2018-08-29 15:03:27.9800000,2018-08-29
2,Sudhir,Senior Software Engineer,CSE-CTE,2018-08-29 15:03:27.9800000
3,Gandhali,Software Engineer Manager,CSE-CTE,2018-08-29 15:03:27.9800
4,Shweta,Software Engineer Manager,CSE-CTE,2018-08-29 15:03:27.9800000
5,Mani,Senior Software Engineer,CSE-EE,2018-08-29 15:03:27.9800000,20
```

📓 Booksa85bf2b5-5168-4486-9aec-8e5436443de5.txt - Notepad   —   □   ✕

File   Edit   Format   View   Help

```
1,Microsoft Azure,Computers,125.60,2018-08-29 18:29:01.3800000
2,Advanced AI,Statistics,172.56,2018-08-29 18:29:01.3800000
3,Asp.Net 4 Blue Book,Programming,56.00,2018-08-29 18:29:01.3800000
4,Visual Studio Code,Programming,99.99,2018-08-29 18:29:01.3800000
```

Figure 6-60. *Azure Data Factory output*

61) Check the e-mail account; you should see an e-mail like in Figure 6-61.

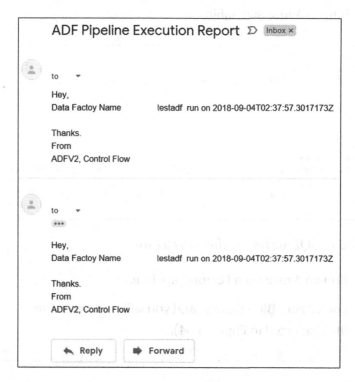

Figure 6-61. *Azure Data Factory pipeline execution report e-mail*

62) In Azure SQL Server, check the WatermarkValue config table (see Figure 6-62).

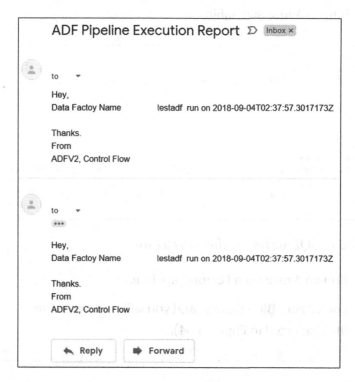

Figure 6-62. *Watermark value update*

Let's insert some more records in the tables.

1) Run the code shown in Figure 6-63 to insert records into an Azure SQL table.

```
--Insert a record in Books table
INSERT INTO dbo.Books
    (BookID,BookName, BookCategory, BookPrice,RecordModifiedDate)
VALUES
    (5,'Operationalize ADF Pipeline', 'Computers', 525.6, GETDATE())
GO

--Insert a record in Employee table
INSERT INTO Employee
    (EmpID, EmpName, EmpDesignation, EmpDepartment, EmpJoining,RecordModifiedDate)
VALUES
    (6, 'Jason', 'Senior Content Writer', 'PG', GETDATE(), GETDATE())
Go
```

Figure 6-63. *SQL script for data insertion*

2) Run an Azure Data Factory pipeline.

3) Look Azure Blob Storage and you will find two more files (selected in Figure 6-64).

Name	Last Modified	Blob Type	Content Type	Size
Booksd0b0888f-c817-4391-ad2a-ce8c4750b857.txt	9/4/2018, 2:16:07 PM	Block Blob	application/octet-stream	76 B
Employeed0b0888f-c817-4391-ad2a-ce8c4750b857.txt	9/4/2018, 2:16:07 PM	Block Blob	application/octet-stream	90 B
Booksa85bf2b5-5168-4486-9aec-8e5436443de5.txt	9/4/2018, 12:38:23 PM	Block Blob	application/octet-stream	262 B
Employeea85bf2b5-5168-4486-9aec-8e5436443de5.txt	9/4/2018, 12:38:22 PM	Block Blob	application/octet-stream	484 B

Figure 6-64. *Azure Data Factory output*

4) Open the files to see the new data (see Figure 6-65).

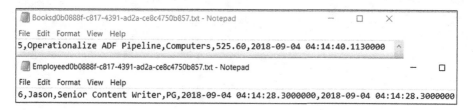

Figure 6-65. *Azure Data Factory output data*

5) Check the watermark values in the config table (see
Figure 6-66).

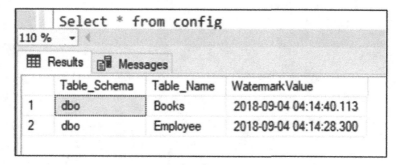

Figure 6-66. *Watermark value update*

You built a solution to understand how the flow can be handled within
Azure Data Factory. There are other functions and activities that can be
used on a case-by-case basis.

Summary

In this chapter, you learned about managing the data pipeline flow and
learned how to use expressions, functions, and activities to control the data
flow in Azure Data Factory.

CHAPTER 7

Security

Data is both an asset and a potential liability. As we move data to the cloud, it becomes highly important to understand the various stages that the data goes through so you can understand the security risks and plan mitigations in case of issues. In this chapter, you will investigate the various security mechanisms that Azure Data Factory provides to secure your data.

Overview

Azure Data Factory management resources are built on the Azure security infrastructure, and they use all the possible security measures offered by Azure. Azure Data Factory does not store any data except for the metadata information such as the pipeline, the activity, and in some cases the linked service credentials (connections to data stores) that are using the Azure integration runtime and are encrypted and stored on ADF managed storage.

Azure Data Factory has been certified for the following: HIPAA/HITECH, ISO/IEC 27001, ISO/IEC 27018, CSA STAR.

If you're interested in Azure compliance and how Azure secures its own infrastructure, visit the Microsoft Trust Center (http://aka.ms/azuretrust).

This chapter will cover authentication, credential management, data security in transit and at rest, and network security, as well as both on-premises to cloud (hybrid) and cloud to cloud scenarios (Figure 7-1).

© Sudhir Rawat and Abhishek Narain 2019
S. Rawat and A. Narain, *Understanding Azure Data Factory*,
https://doi.org/10.1007/978-1-4842-4122-6_7

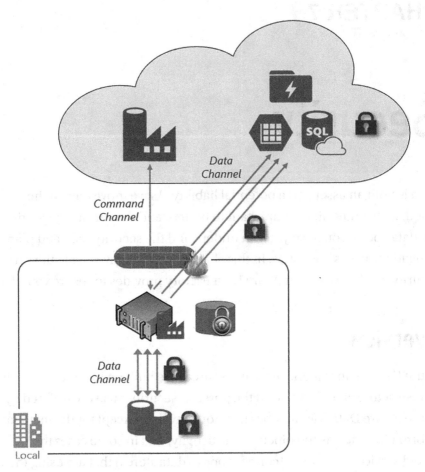

Figure 7-1. *Data channel and command channel in ADF. The data channel is used for the actual data movement, while the command channel is required only for communication within the ADF service.*

Cloud scenario: In this scenario, both your source
and your destination are publicly accessible through
the Internet. These include managed cloud storage
services such as Azure Storage, Azure SQL Data
Warehouse, Azure SQL Database, Azure Data Lake
Store, Amazon S3, Amazon Redshift, SaaS services
such as Salesforce, and web protocols such as

FTP and OData. Find a complete list of supported data sources at https://docs.microsoft.com/en-us/azure/data-factory/copy-activity-overview#supported-data-stores-and-formats.

Hybrid scenario: In this scenario, either your source or your destination is behind a firewall or inside an on-premises corporate network. Or, the data store is in a private network or virtual network (most often the source) and is not publicly accessible. Database servers hosted on virtual machines also fall under this scenario.

Cloud Scenario

This section explains the cloud scenario.

Securing the Data Credentials

Let's begin with securing the data store credentials (Figure 7-2).

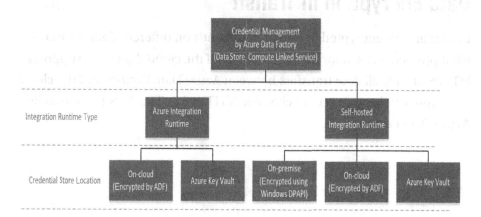

Figure 7-2. *Data store credential storage options in ADF*

- Store the encrypted credentials in an Azure Data Factory managed store. Azure Data Factory helps protect your data store credentials by encrypting them with certificates managed by Microsoft. These certificates are rotated every two years (which includes certificate renewal and the migration of credentials). The encrypted credentials are securely stored in an Azure storage account managed by Azure Data Factory management services. For more information about Azure Storage security, see the Azure Storage security overview at `https://docs.microsoft.com/en-us/ azure/security/security-storage-overview`.

- You can also store the data store's credentials in Azure Key Vault. Azure Data Factory retrieves the credentials during the execution of an activity. For more information, see `https://docs.microsoft.com/ en-us/azure/data-factory/store-credentials-in- key-vault`.

Data Encryption in Transit

Data is always encrypted in transit. It depends on different data stores on what protocol is used for the connectivity. If the cloud data store supports HTTPS or TLS, all data transfers between Azure Data Factory and the cloud data store will be via a secure channel of HTTPS or TLS. TLS 1.2 is used by Azure Data Factory.

Data Encryption at Rest

Azure Data Factory relies on the corresponding data stores to keep your data encrypted. ADF recommends enabling a data encryption mechanism for the data stores that support it.

- *Azure SQL Data Warehouse*: This supports Transparent Data Encryption (TDE), which helps protect against the threat of malicious activity by performing real-time encryption and decryption of your data. This behavior is transparent to the client.

- *Azure SQL Database*: Azure SQL Database supports TDE, which helps protect against the threat of malicious activity by performing real-time encryption and decryption of the data, without requiring changes to the application. This behavior is transparent to the client.

- *Azure Storage*: Azure Blob Storage and Azure Table Storage support Storage Service Encryption (SSE), which automatically encrypts your data before persisting to storage and decrypts it before retrieval.

- *Azure Data Lake Store (Gen1/ Gen2)*: Azure Data Lake Store provides encryption for data stored in the account. When encryption is enabled, Azure Data Lake Store automatically encrypts the data before persisting and decrypts it before retrieval, making it transparent to the client that accesses the data.

- *Amazon S3*: This provides the encryption of data at rest for both the client and the server.

- *Amazon Redshift*: This supports cluster encryption for data at rest.

- *Azure Cosmos DB*: This supports the encryption of data at rest and is automatically applied for both new and existing customers in all Azure regions. There is no need to configure anything.

- *Salesforce*: Salesforce supports Shield Platform Encryption, which allows encryption of all files, attachments, and custom fields.

Hybrid Scenario

Hybrid scenarios require the self-hosted integration runtime to be installed in an on-premises network, inside a virtual network (Azure), or inside a virtual private cloud (Amazon). The self-hosted integration runtime (Figure 7-3) must be able to access the local data stores. For more information about the self-hosted integration runtime, see `https://docs.microsoft.com/azure/data-factory/create-self-hosted-integration-runtime`.

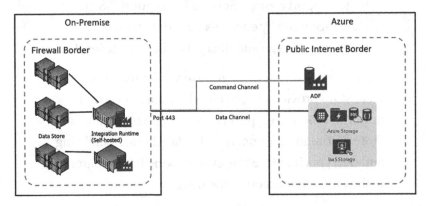

Figure 7-3. *Hybrid setup using the self-hosted integration runtime to connect on-premise data stores*

The command channel allows for communication between data movement services in Azure Data Factory and the self-hosted integration runtime. The communication contains information related to the activity. The data channel is used for transferring data between on-premise data stores and cloud data stores.

On-Premise Data Store Credentials

The credentials for your on-premise data stores are always encrypted and stored. They can be either stored locally on the self-hosted integration runtime machine or stored in Azure Data Factory managed storage.

You can also use Azure Key Vault and reference the keys/secrets in Azure Data Factory. This helps in building a centralized credential store for all apps and reduces the manageability.

- Store credentials locally. The self-hosted integration runtime uses Windows DPAPI to encrypt the sensitive data and credential information.

- Store credentials in Azure Data Factory managed storage. If you directly use the Set-AzureRmDataFactoryV2LinkedService cmdlet with the connection strings and credentials inline in the JSON, the linked service is encrypted and stored in Azure Data Factory managed storage. The sensitive information is still encrypted by certificates, and Microsoft manages these certificates.

- Store credentials in Azure Key Vault (AKV). Credentials stored in AKV are fetched by ADF during runtime.

Figure 7-4 shows the options.

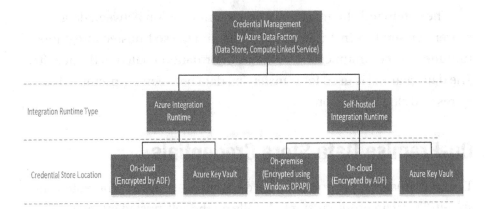

Figure 7-4. *Data store credential storage options in ADF*

Encryption in Transit

All data transfers are via the secure channel of HTTPS and TLS over TCP to prevent man-in-the-middle attacks during communication with Azure services.

You can also use an IPSec VPN or Azure ExpressRoute to further secure the communication channel between your on-premise network and Azure.

Azure Virtual Network is a logical representation of your network in the cloud. You can connect an on-premise network to your virtual network by setting up an IPSec VPN (site-to-site) or ExpressRoute (private peering).

Table 7-1 summarizes the network and self-hosted integration runtime configuration recommendations based on different combinations of source and destination locations for hybrid data movement.

Table 7-1. *Network and Self-Hosted Integration Runtime Configuration*

Source	Destination	Network Configuration	Integration Runtime Setup
On-premises	Virtual machines and cloud services deployed in virtual networks	IPSec VPN (point-to-site or site-to-site)	The self-hosted integration runtime can be installed either on-premises or on an Azure virtual machine in a virtual network.
On-premises	Virtual machines and cloud services deployed in virtual networks	ExpressRoute (private peering)	The self-hosted integration runtime can be installed either on-premises or on an Azure virtual machine in a virtual network.
On-premises	Azure-based services that have a public endpoint	ExpressRoute (public peering)	The self-hosted integration runtime must be installed on-premises.

Figure 7-5 and Figure 7-6 show the use of the self-hosted integration runtime for moving data between an on-premises database and Azure services by using ExpressRoute and IPSec VPN (with Azure Virtual Network).

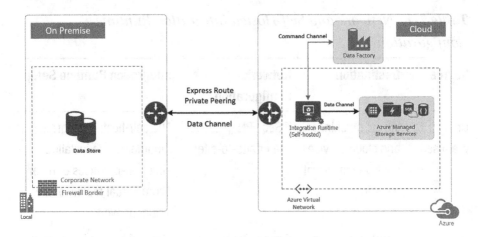

Figure 7-5. *Express route network setup for accessing on-premise data stores*

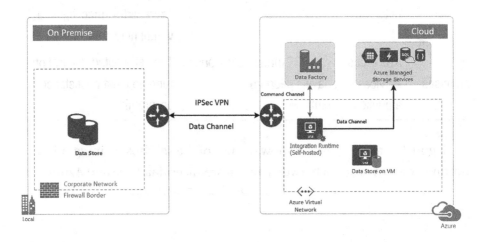

Figure 7-6. *IPSec VPN setup for accessing the on-premise data stores*

Considerations for Selecting Express Route or VPN

Express Route is a better choice as it is safer and gives you dedicated bandwidth, at an additional cost.

The self-hosted IR can be set up either on-premises or on an Azure VM to access your data stores. I personally prefer setting it up on an Azure VM for the ease of manageability and network setup.

If you set up the self-hosted IR on-premises, then you need to grant access from your on-premises networks to your storage account/data sources with an IP network rule. In addition, you must identify the Internet-facing IP addresses used by your network. If your network is connected to the Azure network using ExpressRoute, each circuit is configured with two public IP addresses at the Microsoft edge that are used to connect to Microsoft services like Azure Storage using Azure public peering. To allow communication from your circuit to Azure Storage, you must create IP network rules for the public IP addresses of your circuits. To find your ExpressRoute circuit's public IP addresses, open a support ticket with ExpressRoute via the Azure portal.

Firewall Configurations and IP Whitelisting for Self-Hosted Integration Runtime Functionality

In an enterprise, a corporate firewall runs on the central router of the organization. Windows Firewall runs as a daemon on the local machine in which the self-hosted integration runtime is installed (Figure 7-7).

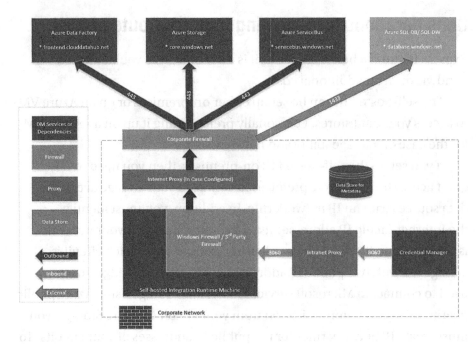

Figure 7-7. *Firewall configurations and IP whitelisting requirements*

Table 7-2 provides outbound port and domain requirements for corporate firewalls.

Table 7-2. *Outbound Port and Domain Requirements*

Domain Names	Outbound Ports	Description
*.servicebus.windows.net	443	Required by the self-hosted integration runtime to connect to data movement services in Azure Data Factory.
*.frontend.clouddatahub.net	443	Required by the self-hosted integration runtime to connect to the Azure Data Factory service.
download.microsoft.com	443	Required by the self-hosted integration runtime for downloading the updates. If you have disabled auto-updates, then you may skip this.
*.core.windows.net	443	Used by the self-hosted integration runtime to connect to the Azure storage account when you use the copy feature.
*.database.windows.net	1433	(Optional) Required when you copy from or to Azure SQL Database or Azure SQL Data Warehouse. Use the staged copy feature to copy data to Azure SQL Database or Azure SQL Data Warehouse without opening port 1433.

(continued)

Table 7-2. (*continued*)

Domain Names	Outbound Ports	Description
`*.azuredatalakestore.` `netlogin.microsoftonline.` `com/<tenant>/oauth2/token`	443	(Optional) Required when you copy from or to Azure Data Lake Store.
`download.microsoft.com`	443	Used for downloading the updates.

At the Windows firewall level (in other words, the machine level), these outbound ports are normally enabled. If not, you can configure the domains and ports accordingly on the self-hosted integration runtime machine. Port 8060 is required for node-to-node communication in the self-hosted IR when you have set up high availability (two or more nodes).

IP Configurations and Whitelisting in Data Stores

Some data stores in the cloud also require that you whitelist the IP address of the machine accessing the store. Ensure that the IP address of the self-hosted integration runtime machine is whitelisted or configured in the firewall appropriately.

Proxy Server Considerations

If your corporate network environment uses a proxy server to access the Internet, configure the self-hosted integration runtime to use the appropriate proxy settings (see Figure 7-8). You can set the proxy during the initial registration phase.

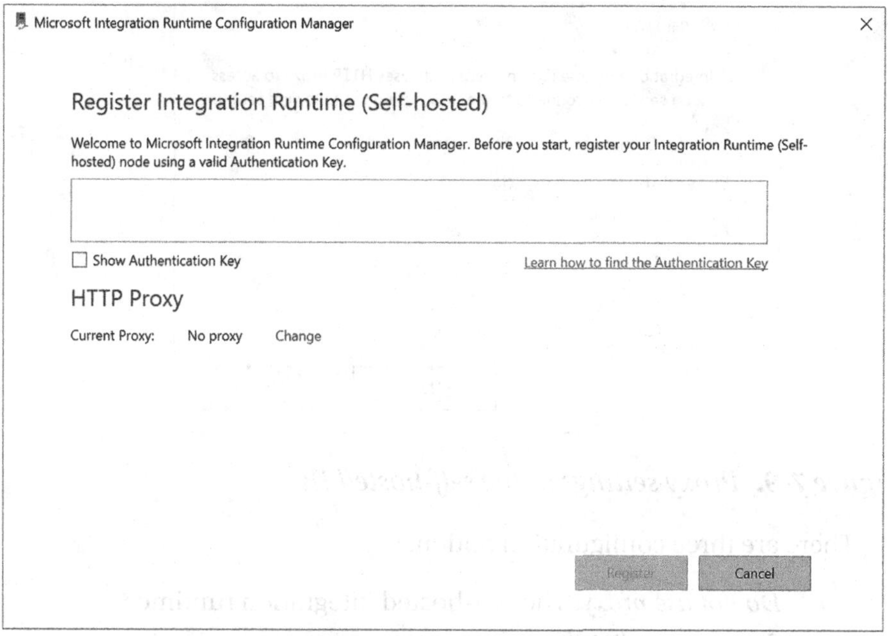

Figure 7-8. *Self-hosted IR configuration manager*

The self-hosted integration runtime uses the proxy server to connect to the cloud service. Click the Change link during the initial setup. You will see the proxy setting dialog (see Figure 7-9).

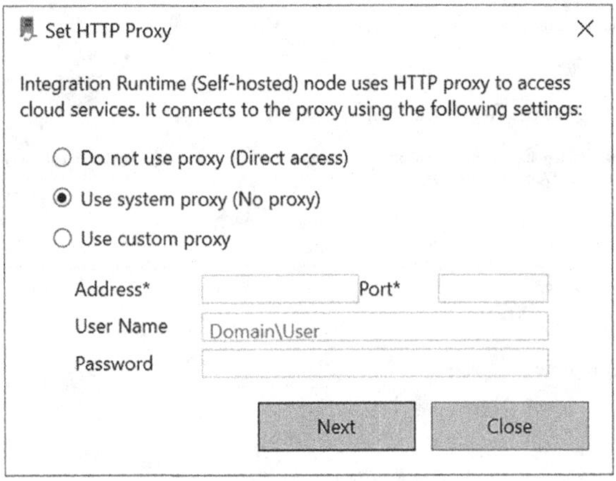

Figure 7-9. Proxy settings in the self-hosted IR

There are three configuration options:

- *Do not use proxy*: The self-hosted integration runtime does not explicitly use any proxy to connect to cloud services.

- *Use system proxy*: The self-hosted integration runtime uses the proxy setting that is configured in `diahost.exe.config` and `diawp.exe.config`. If no proxy is configured in `diahost.exe.config` and `diawp.exe.config`, the self-hosted integration runtime connects to the cloud service directly without going through a proxy.

- *Use custom proxy*: Configure the HTTP proxy setting to use the self-hosted integration runtime, instead of using configurations in `diahost.exe.config` and `diawp.exe.config`. The Address and Port fields are required. The User Name and Password fields are optional depending on your proxy's authentication setting. All settings are encrypted with Windows DPAPI on the self-hosted integration runtime and stored locally on the machine.

The integration runtime host service restarts automatically after you save the updated proxy settings. This is an HTTP proxy; hence, only connections involving HTTP/ HTTPS use the proxy, whereas database connections will not use the proxy.

Storing Credentials in Azure Key Vault

You can store credentials for data stores and computes in Azure Key Vault. Azure Data Factory retrieves the credentials when executing an activity that uses the data store/compute.

Prerequisites

This feature relies on the Azure Data Factory service identity.

In Azure Key Vault, when you create a secret, use the entire value of the secret property that the ADF linked service asks for (e.g., connection string/ password/service principal key, and so on). For example, for the Azure Storage linked service, enter DefaultEndpointsProtocol=http;AccountNa me=myAccount;AccountKey=myKey; as the AKV secret for myPassword. Then reference it in the connectionString field in ADF. For the Dynamics linked service, enter myPassword as the AKV secret and then reference it in the Password field in ADF. All ADF connectors support AKV.

Steps

To reference a credential stored in Azure Key Vault, you need to do the following:

1. Retrieve the data factory service identity by copying the value of Service Identity Application ID that is generated with your factory. If you use the ADF authoring UI, the service identity ID will be shown

in the Azure Key Vault linked service creation window. You can also retrieve it from the Azure portal; refer to `https://docs.microsoft.com/en-us/azure/data-factory/data-factory-service-identity#retrieve-service-identity`.

2. Grant the service identity access to your Azure Key Vault. In Key Vault, go to "Access policies," click "Add new," and search for this service identity application ID to grant Get permission to in the "Secret permissions" drop-down. This allows this designated factory to access the secret in Key Vault.

3. Create a linked service pointing to your Azure Key Vault. Refer to `https://docs.microsoft.com/en-us/azure/data-factory/store-credentials-in-key-vault#azure-key-vault-linked-service`.

4. Create a data store linked service, inside which you can reference the corresponding secret stored in Key Vault.

Using the Authoring UI

Click Connections, click Linked Services, and then click "+ New." Search for *Azure Key Vault* (Figure 7-10).

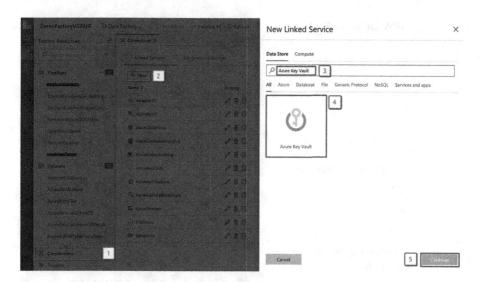

Figure 7-10. *Creating an Azure Key Vault linked service for connecting to a Key Vault account for pulling the credentials in during execution time*

Select the provisioned Azure Key Vault where your credentials are stored. You can click "Test connection" to make sure your AKV connection is valid (Figure 7-11).

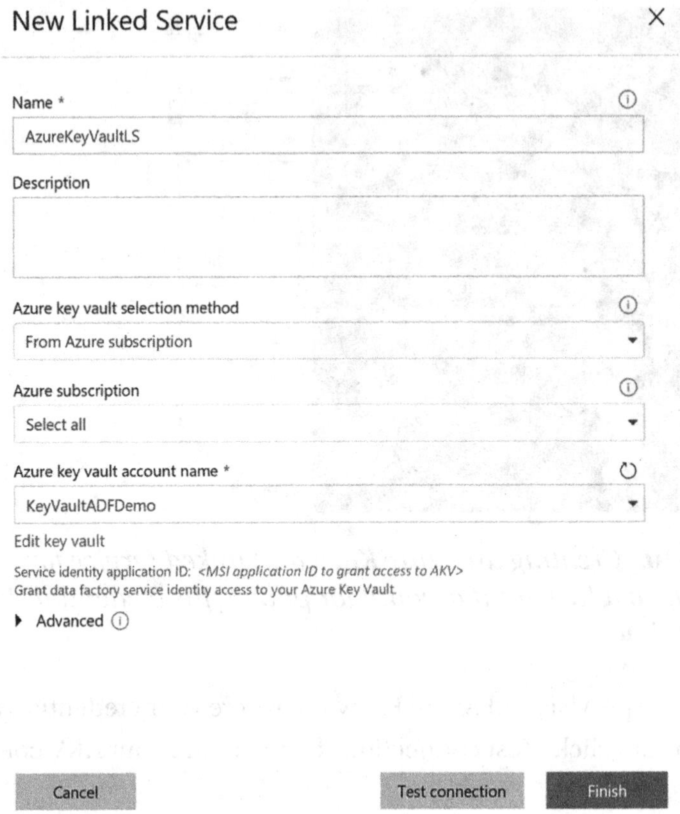

New Linked Service   ✕

Name *   ⓘ

AzureKeyVaultLS

Description

Azure key vault selection method   ⓘ

From Azure subscription   ▾

Azure subscription   ⓘ

Select all   ▾

Azure key vault account name *   ↻

KeyVaultADFDemo   ▾

Edit key vault

Service identity application ID: <MSI application ID to grant access to AKV>
Grant data factory service identity access to your Azure Key Vault.

▶ Advanced ⓘ

Cancel   Test connection   Finish

Figure 7-11. *Key Vault linked service properties*

Here's the JSON representation of the AKV linked service:

```
{
    "name": "AzureKeyVaultLinkedService",
    "properties": {
        "type": "AzureKeyVault",
        "typeProperties": {
            "baseUrl": "https://<azureKeyVaultName>.vault.azure.net"
        }
    }
}
```

Reference Secret Stored in Key Vault

The properties shown in Table 7-3 are supported when you configure a field in the linked service referencing a key vault secret.

Table 7-3. *Properties*

Property	Description	Required
type	The type property of the field must be set to AzureKeyVaultSecret.	Yes
secretName	The name of the secret in Azure Key Vault.	Yes
secretVersion	The version of the secret in Azure Key Vault.If not specified, it always uses the latest version of the secret.If specified, then it sticks to the given version.	No
store	Refers to an Azure Key Vault linked service that you use to store the credential.	Yes

Using the Authoring UI

Select Azure Key Vault for secret fields while creating the connection to your data store/compute. Select the provisioned Azure Key Vault linked service and provide the secret name. You can optionally provide a secret version (see Figure 7-12).

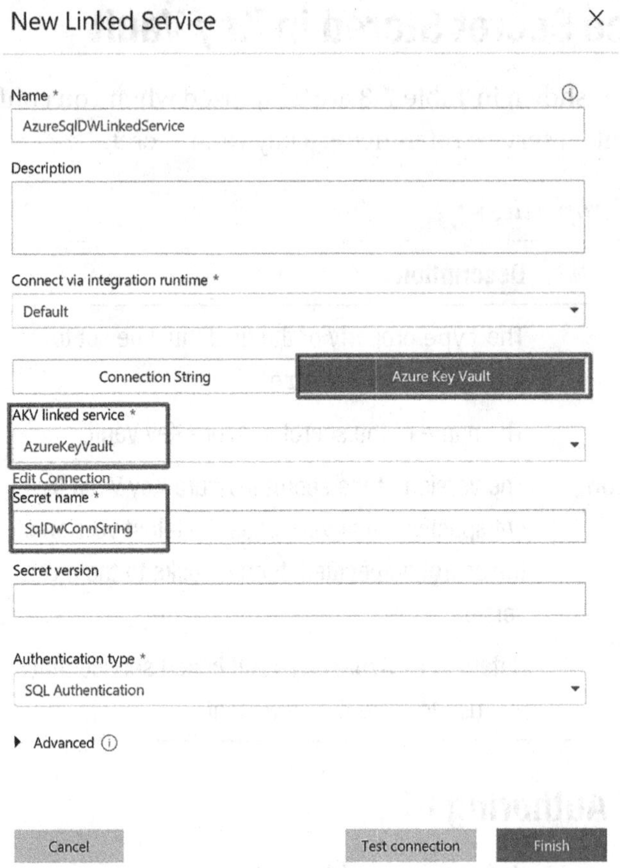

Figure 7-12. *SQL DW linked service referencing the secret from Azure Key Vault*

Here's the JSON (see the password section):

```
{
    "name": "DynamicsLinkedService",
    "properties": {
        "type": "Dynamics",
        "typeProperties": {
            "deploymentType": "<>",
            "organizationName": "<>",
            "authenticationType": "<>",
            "username": "<>",
            "password": {
                "type": "AzureKeyVaultSecret",
                "secretName": "<secret name in AKV>",
                "store":{
                    "referenceName": "<Azure Key Vault linked service>",
                    "type": "LinkedServiceReference"
                }
            }
        }
    }
}
```

Figure 7-13. *JSON representation of a linked service that references secrets/passwords from Key Vault using the Azure Key Vault linked service*

Advanced Security with Managed Service Identity

When creating an Azure Data Factory instance, a service identity can be created along with factory creation. The service identity is a managed application registered to Azure Activity Directory and represents this specific Azure Data Factory.

The Data Factory service identity gives you the following benefits:

- You can store the credentials in Azure Key Vault, in which case the Azure Data Factory service identity is used for Azure Key Vault authentication.

- It has many connectors including Azure Blob Storage, Azure Data Lake Storage Gen1, Azure SQL Database, and Azure SQL Data Warehouse.

A common problem is how to manage the final keys. For example, even if you store the keys/secrets in Azure Key Vault, you need to create another secret to access Key Vault (let's say using a service principal in Azure Active Directory).

Managed Service Identity (MSI) helps you build a secret-free ETL pipeline on Azure. The less you expose the secrets/credentials to data engineers/users, the safer they are. This really eases the tough job of credential management for the data engineers. This is one of the coolest features of Azure Data Factory.

Summary

In any cloud solution, security plays an important role. Often the security teams will have questions about the architecture before they approve the product/service in question to be used. The objective of this chapter was to expose you to all the security requirements when using ADF.

We know that most data breaches happen because of leaking data store credentials. With ADF, you can build an end-to-end data pipeline that is password free using technologies like Managed Service Identity. You can create a trust with ADF MSI in your data stores, and ADF can authenticate itself to access the data, completely removing the need to type passwords into ADF!

CHAPTER 8

Executing SSIS Packages

This chapter will focus on how Azure Data Factory makes it possible to run SQL Server Integration Services (SSIS) packages. If you are new to SSIS, then you can skip this chapter; however, if you have an existing SSIS package to migrate or think your customer will ask you to work on SSIS, then it's worth reading this chapter.

Why SSIS Packages?

Back when all data was scattered in different places such as RDBMSs, Excel, third-party sources, and so on, SSIS was the product that was used for data transformation. SSIS is part of the SQL Server family. Developers use it to build data transformation packages to bring all the data into place, massage it, and then provide one version of the truth across the organization. In fact, this tool is very dear to BI developers. If you have ever gotten a chance to work with SSIS, you know what I am talking about.

When the cloud technologies emerged, the number of data sources started to increase. The situation demanded more data drivers, more compute, and a more secure way to process such data. It's never been impossible for any organization to build a massive infrastructure and solution. The question is just whether the organization wants to invest

© Sudhir Rawat and Abhishek Narain 2019
S. Rawat and A. Narain, *Understanding Azure Data Factory*,
https://doi.org/10.1007/978-1-4842-4122-6_8

the time and resources to build that or use the cloud and be ready with a solution in no time. Microsoft Azure introduced Azure Data Factory (ADF), which can scale to any size and allow data transformations from various cloud sources.

But what about the SSIS packages you developed? Do you need to delete those packages and create an ADF pipeline from scratch? Are all the previous efforts wasted?

The answer is no. ADF provides an option to BI/data developers to run SSIS packages on the cloud. This is called the "lift and shift" of SSIS packages. Without much effort, you can run your existing SSIS packages in a managed Azure compute environment.

However, if you are starting to build a data transformation solution, then use Azure Data Factory to build the solution.

Let's get started with a use case.

AdventureWorks wants to leverage cloud compute to run its existing SSIS package. It's time- and resource-consuming for AdventureWorks to rewrite the entire package logic in ADF. So, the company decided to leverage ADF's SSIS lift and shift feature. You'll use a basic SSIS package and complete this via the following steps:

1) Provision Azure SQL Server Database or SQL Server Managed Instance to host SSIDB.

2) Provision the Azure-SSIS IR via the Azure portal, PowerShell, and the Azure Resource Manager template.

3) Deploy the SSIS package via SQL Server Management Studio (SSMS), SQL Server Data Tools, the command-line interface (CLI), custom code/ PSH using SSIS Managed Object Model (MOM) .NET SDK/API, and T-SQL scripts executing SSISDB processes.

4)   Execute SSIS packages through SSMS, the CLI by
running dtexec.exe, custom code/PSH using SSIS
MOM .NET SDK/API, and T-SQL scripts executing
SSISDB processes.

If you want to monitor SSIS package executions, then you can do so via
the Azure portal, PowerShell, and SSMS.

Let's start setting up the environment to run SSIS packages on
ADF. Figure 8-1 shows the SSIS package you'll be shifting to Azure.

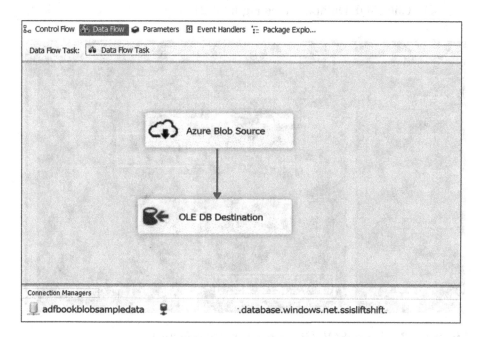

Figure 8-1. *Sample SSIS package*

Provision the Azure SQL Server Database

As mentioned earlier, the first step is to set up Azure SQL Server Database to host SSISDB.

1) Go to https://portal.azure.com.

2) Click "Create a resource."

3) Click Databases.

4) Click SQL Database (see Figure 8-2).

Figure 8-2. *Azure SQL Database service selection*

5) Provide the database name.

6) Select your subscription.

7) Select or create a new resource group.

8) Select "Blank database" for "Select source."

9) Select or create a new server.

10) Select "Yes/Not now" for "Want to use SQL elastic pool."

11) Select your needed pricing tier or leave it at the default.

12) Leave the default value for Collation.

13) Click Create (see Figure 8-3).

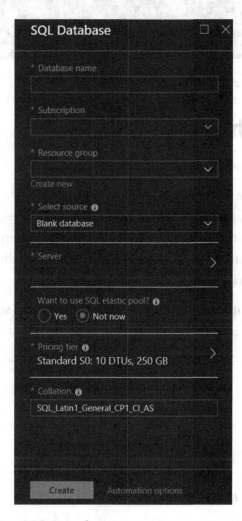

Figure 8-3. *Azure SQL Database setup*

14) Monitor the notifications to check the progress (see Figure 8-4).

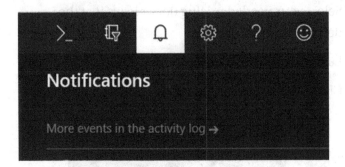

Figure 8-4. *Azure activity notifications*

Provision the Azure-SSIS IR

The next step is to set up the Azure-SSIS IR.

1) From the Azure portal, click Azure Data Factory Services, and click Author & Monitor. If you haven't created an Azure Data Factory instance yet, then please refer to the previous chapters to set up the ADF service.

2) In the Author & Monitor UI, click Connection (see Figure 8-5).

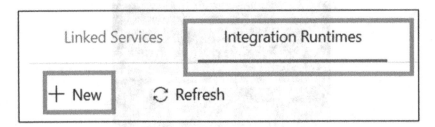

Figure 8-5. *New integration runtime*

3) Select "Lift-and-shift existing SSIS packages to execute in Azure" and click Next (see Figure 8-6).

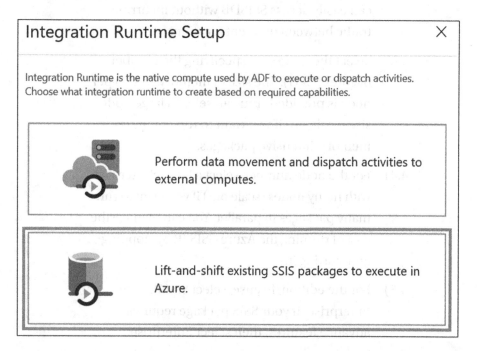

Figure 8-6. *Choosing an SSIS-IR option*

4) Configure Integration Runtime Setup.

4.1) Provide a name and description, and specify Azure-SSIS for Type.

4.2) Select the right location for the Azure-SSIS IR to achieve high performance in ETL workflows. It doesn't need to be the same the location as ADFv2. It should be the same as the location of the Azure SQL DB/MI server where SSISDB will be hosted or the location of VNet connected to an on-premise network. Avoid the Azure-SSIS IR accessing SSISDB/

data movements across different locations.
This way, your Azure-SSIS integration runtime
can easily access SSISDB without incurring
traffic between different locations.

4.3)   Select the node size, specifying the number
of cores (CPU). The size of memory (RAM) per
node is provided. You can select a large node
size (scale up) if you want to run compute/
memory-intensive packages.

4.4)   For the node number, select a large cluster
with many nodes (scale out) if you want to run
many packages in parallel. You can manage the
cost of running the Azure-SSIS IR by stopping
and starting it.

4.5)   For the edition/license, select Standard or
Enterprise. If your SSIS package requires
advance features, then select Enterprise.

4.6)   For Save Money, bring your own SQL Server
license to save money (see Figure 8-7).

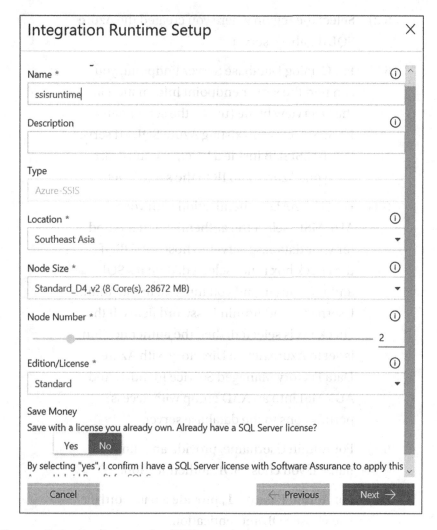

Figure 8-7. Setting up the SSIS runtime

5)   Click Next.

6)   Configure Integration Runtime Setup.

   6.1)   Select the subscription in which you created
          the Azure SQL database server.

6.2)   Select the region where you created the Azure SQL database server.

6.3)   For Catalog Database Server Endpoint, you can find the server endpoint information in the Overview blade (under the server name). If you select your existing Azure SQL MI server to host SSISDB inside a VNet, you must also join your Azure-SSIS IR to the same VNet.

6.4)   For "Use AAD authentication with your ADF MSI," select the authentication method for your database server to host SSISDB. If the check box is not selected, then it's SQL authentication, and you must fill in the Admin Username and Admin Password fields. If the checkbox is selected, then the authentication is set to Azure Active Directory with Azure Data Factory Managed Service Identity. Add ADF MSI into an AAD group with access permissions to the database server.

6.5)   For Admin Username, provide an admin name if you chose SQL authentication.

6.6)   For Admin Password , provide a password if you chose SQL authentication.

6.7)   For Catalog Database Service Tier, select a database tier of Azure SQL where you want to host SSISDB (see Figure 8-8).

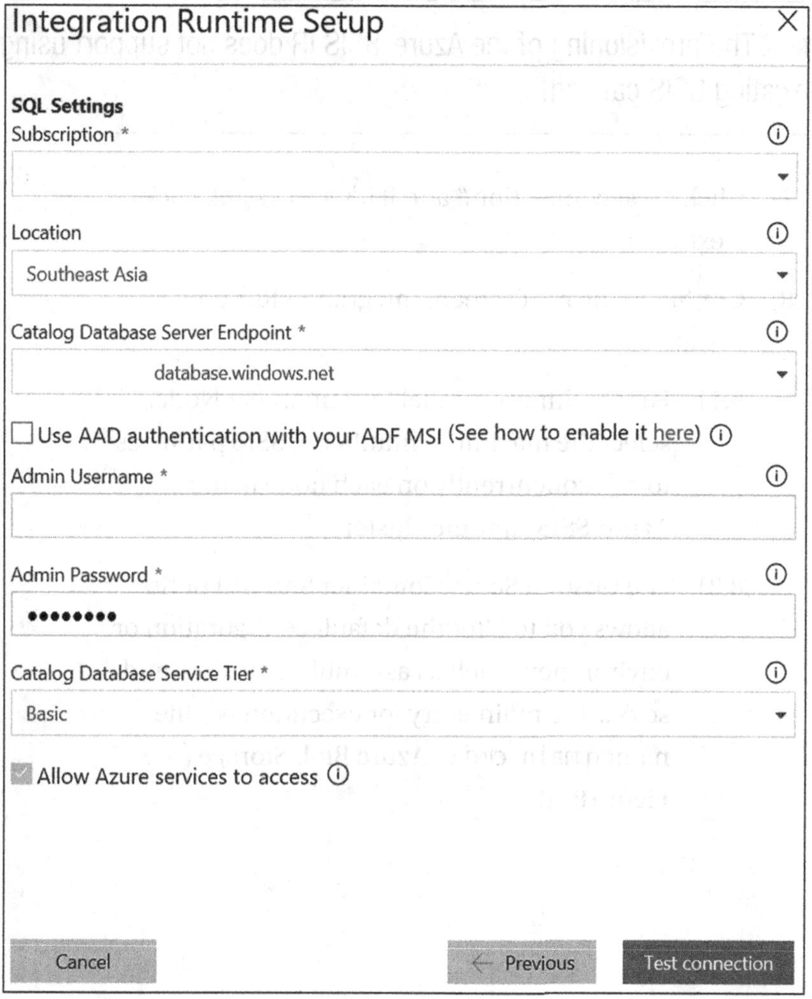

Figure 8-8. *Server options to host SSIS DB*

Note   The provisioning of the Azure-SSIS IR does not support using an existing SSIS catalog.

7) Click "Test connection," and if it's successful, click Next.

8) Configure the next screen, Integration Runtime Setup.

8.1) For Maximum Parallel Execution Per Node, select the maximum number of SSIS packages to run concurrently on each node in the Azure-SSIS runtime cluster.

8.2) The Custom Setup Container SAS URI option allows you to alter the default configuration or environment such as assemblies, drivers, and so on. The main entry for execution is a file named `main.cmd` in Azure Blob Storage (see Figure 8-9).

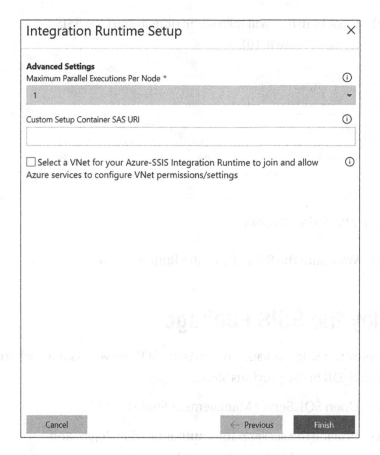

Figure 8-9. *Configuring the load for each node*

8.3)   Select "Select a VNet" if you want the SSIS-IR
to join a virtual network. This is a mandatory
option if you have Azure SQL Database or SQL
MI (managed instance) in a virtual network so
you can host SSISDB or access on-premises
data sources.

9) Click Finish. It will take some time to start the SSIS-IR (see Figure 8-10).

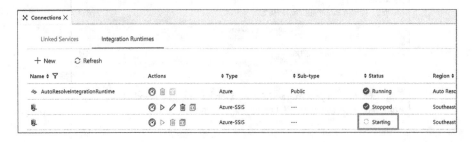

Figure 8-10. *SSIS-IR monitor*

10) Wait until the SSIS-IR has the Running state.

Deploy the SSIS Package

Let's deploy the SSIS package on the Azure SQL Server instance where you hosted SSIS-DB in the previous steps.

1) Open SQL Server Management Studio.

2) Provide the server name, authentication, login, and password. Click Options (see Figure 8-11).

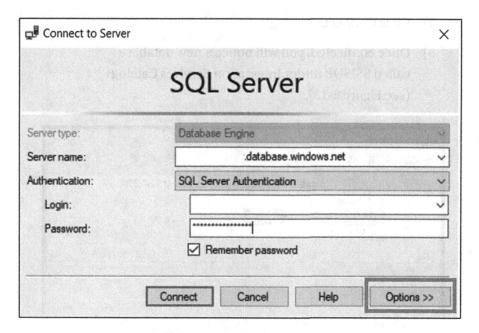

Figure 8-11. *SQL Server Management Studio*

3) On the Connection Properties tab, provide SSISDB
   for "Connect to database" (see Figure 8-12).

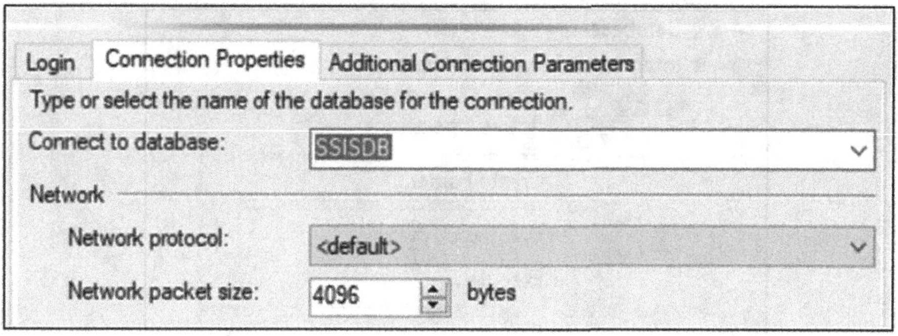

Figure 8-12. *Database selection*

4) Click Connect.

5) Once connected, you will notice a new database
    called SSISDB under Integration Services Catalogs
    (see Figure 8-13).

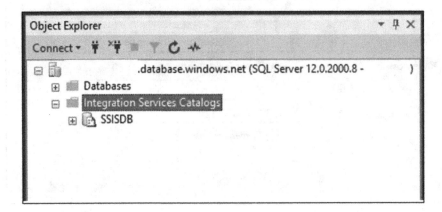

Figure 8-13. *Integration Service Catalogs list*

6) Right-click SSISDB and click Create Folder. I named
    it ssisliftshift (see Figure 8-14).

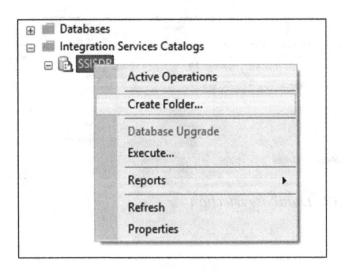

Figure 8-14. *Create Folder option in SSISDB*

7) Once the folder is created, expand the newly created folder and click Deploy Project (see Figure 8-15).

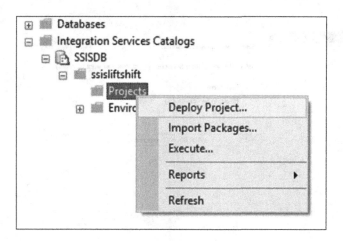

Figure 8-15. *Deploy Project option*

8) On the Introduction page, click Next.

9) On the Select Source page, choose the path where you have the .ispac file (see Figure 8-16).

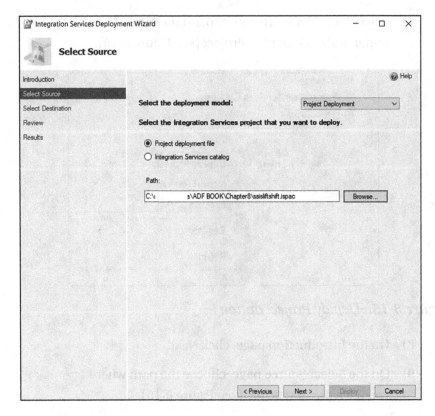

Figure 8-16. *SSIS deployment wizard, selecting the source option*

10) Click Next. You may get a warning message that
the SSIS package is created on a different machine
because of sensitive information such as passwords
stored in the package.

11) Provide the server name where SSISDB is hosted.
Provide the authentication, login, and password
details. Click Connect (see Figure 8-17).

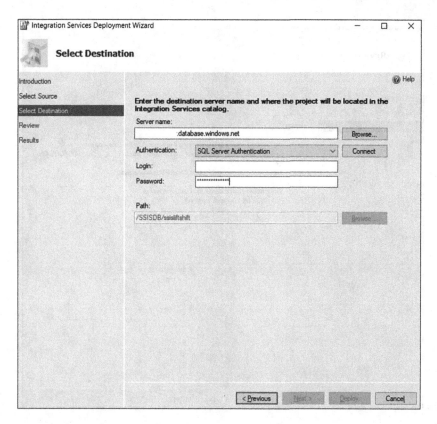

Figure 8-17. SSIS deployment wizard, selecting a destination option

12)   Click Next.

13)   Review your selection and then click Deploy (see
        Figure 8-18).

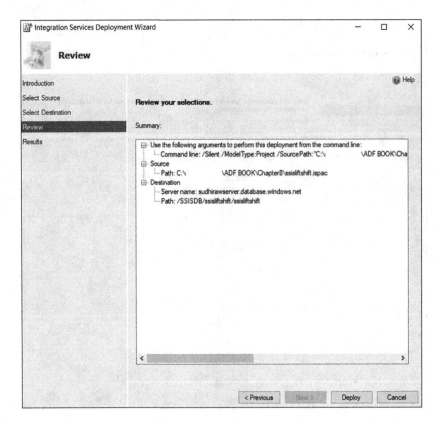

Figure 8-18. *SSIS deployment wizard, reviewing*

14) Once deployment is done, click Close (see Figure 8-19).

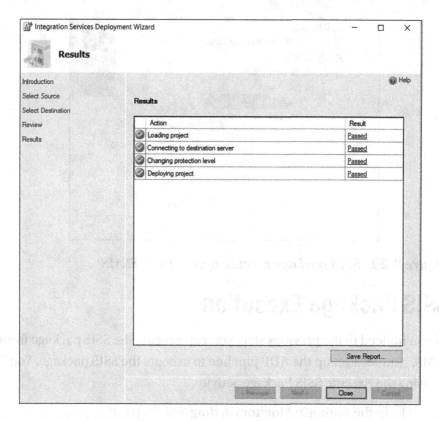

Figure 8-19. *SSIS deployment wizard, deployment progress*

15)   Execute the SSIS package from SSMS, as shown in
       Figure 8-20.

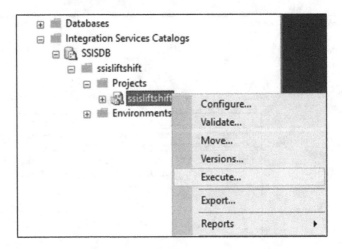

Figure 8-20. *SSIS package execute option from SSMS*

SSIS Package Execution

As you noticed in the previous step, you can execute the SSIS package from SSMS. Now let's set up the ADF pipeline to execute the SSIS package. You'll be using the Execute SSIS Package activity.

1) In the Author & Monitor UI, drag and drop the Execute SSIS Package activity (see Figure 8-21).

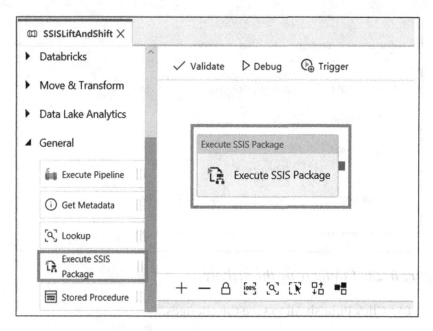

Figure 8-21. *Azure Data Factory activity selection*

2) On the General tab, provide a name and description. Keep the default values for the other properties.

3) On the Settings tab, select the Azure SSIS-IR connection created earlier.

4) Select "32-Bit runtime" if your package requires a 32-bit runtime to execute the package.

5) Select Basic for "Logging level."

6) Provide a package path like FolderName/ ProjectName/PackageName.dtsx.

7) Provide an execution environment path from SSISDB (see Figure 8-22).

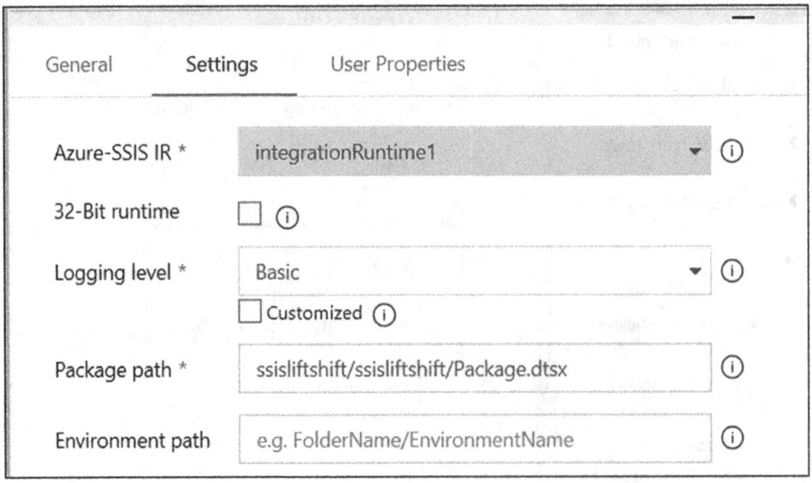

General   Settings   User Properties

Azure-SSIS IR *   integrationRuntime1

32-Bit runtime

Logging level *   Basic
                       ☐ Customized ⓘ

Package path *   ssisliftshift/ssisliftshift/Package.dtsx

Environment path   e.g. FolderName/EnvironmentName

Figure 8-22. *Configuring the activity*

8) Click Publish All to save the changes.

9) Click Trigger and then Trigger Now.

10) Click Monitor to check the progress of the package execution.

Summary

In this chapter, you focused on the SSIS lift and shift feature of ADF. Without investing much time or effort, an organization can use the existing SSIS package in ADF to get the power of cloud compute and security. SSIS-IR makes it possible to run your SSIS packages in a cluster environment.

Index

A

Activities, 7
    control, 24–27
    dependency, 27, 29
    execution, 20–22
    policy, 23–24
Azure Active Directory (AD) app
    adding permission, 107
    ADF connection, 108
    API selection, 177
    Azure Blob Storage, 109–110
    Azure portal, 173
    code file, 184
    creating, 175
    granting permission to user, 179
    HDI creation values, 113
    HDI linked service, 112
    Hive activity, 111, 112
    Hive script path, 114
    keys, 103, 178–179
    member selection, 183
    monitor option, 116
    output, 116
    permission assignment, 181
    permission settings, 176, 178, 181
    properties, 104
    publishing changes, 115

registration, 101–103, 173–174
role options, 180
settings, 175–176
subscriptions, 105, 106
user access, 182
user selection, 180
U-SQL activity, 185–191
values, 104
Azure Batch services
    create resource, 247
    pools
        nodes, 253–254
        setup, 250
        values, 250–253
    prerequisites, 249
    setup, 247–249
    software and packages, virtual
        machine, 249
    storage account, 248
    subscription, 248
Azure Blob Storage, 219
    Azure SQL Database
        input values, 229–230
        linked service, 226–227
        option, 226
    connection, 224, 228–229
    container name and access
        level, 276

P, Q, R

T

Twitter application
  access token, 237–238
  Azure AD app
    keys, 241
    registered, 240
    registration option, 238–239
    registration values, 239–240
    settings, 240
  Azure Batch services (*see* Azure
    Batch services)
  Azure Cosmos DB
    collection, 246
    input values, 243–244, 246
    new database, 245
    services, 244
    setup, 243
    storage capacity, 247
  Azure Key Vault, 241–242
    access policies, 255–257
    Python code, 257–258
    secrets, 254–255
  creating, 236
  settings, 237–238

U, V, W, X, Y, Z

User interface (UI)
  author pipelines, 51
  Azure portal, 42–43
    authoring and monitoring
      data pipelines, 46–47
    creating, Data Factory v2
      instance, 44–45
    Data Factory, 43–44
    launching, 46
  CI/CD workflow, 48–50
  code repository, 47–48
  monitoring data pipelines, 52
  prerequisites, 42
  VSTS release definition, 50–51
U-SQL activity
  code, 185–186
  configuring, 189
  drag and drop, 187
  output, 191
  properties, 190
  script path, 189–190
  setup, 188
  subscription, 188

Printed in the United States
By Bookmasters